The Candlelight Painter

This book is dedicated to
my wife Bridget and our family

The Candlelight Painter

The Life and Work of William Cauley, Traveller, Painter and Poet

Transcribed and edited by Mícheál Ó hAodha

A. & A. Farmar

British Library cataloguing in Publication Data
A CIP catalogue record for this book is available from the British Library.

Photography by Alice Campbell
Edited, designed and set by A. & A. Farmar
Printed and bound in Spain by GraphyCems

ISBN 1-899047-11-5

First published in 2004
by
A. & A. Farmar
Beech House
78 Ranelagh Village
Dublin 6
Ireland
Tel: 353 1 496 3625
Fax: 353 1 497 0107
Email: afarmar@iol.ie
Web: farmarbooks.com

Contents

Acknowledgements

The author, editor and publishers are deeply indebted to a number of individuals and groups for financial support. We are very grateful to the following: John Heneghan, Coordinator of the HEA Travellers' Initiative, University of Limerick; Sandra Joyce and Niall Keegan, Coordinators of the Nomad Project, the Irish World Music Centre, University of Limerick; An Chomhairle Oidhreachta (The Heritage Council of Ireland). We would also like to thank Dessie O'Brien, of the Haven Bar, Limerick, for facilitating the photographing of the paintings.

THE GLIMMER-MAN

by *Siúlach Scéalach**

Wandering
Meandering the streets
Mapping the alleys
Forging new paths
In the journey of the soul

I arrived here
Limerick
A proud city
Hard-edged
Vibrant
A city all its own

And at its centre
A symbol
A battered white caravan
Fenced in and forgotten
Trapped
Fettered
As a cornered animal

Dead, yet alive
Sleeping you could say
Resting
Tamed

*The Irish phrase *Siúlach Scéalach* or '*An té atá siulach bíonn sé scéalach*' means 'the person who walks (travels) far has many stories.'

I heard them then
Those laboured breaths
That strange rhythm,
Pulsing
Expectant
In the heart of the city

I was drawn to it
That life
That beating heart
It was the end of something
The end of the road?
And the beginning of something else.

I moved into the centre
To the very core
I could feel the energy
Of each trace and sinew

He was there
Feverish
Working
Battling
A proud man
A man of war

No one disturbed him
Where he wrestled
His heart lying there
Open
Honest

Spreadeagled
Upon the canvas
I could see each straining muscle
Every beat and sinew

And all the while
The brush swayed
Each stroke a victory
For energy
For light
See him there
The Glimmer-Man
The Candlelight Painter.

Introduction

This book is the life story of William Cauley, painter, poet and singer, as told to Micheál Ó hAodha. Willy is a Traveller who lives on the banks of the Shannon in the heart of Limerick city. He is known to his friends as 'the candlelight painter' because of his unique style of painting. As the father of a large family, he finds night-time the best time in which to work. He therefore sets up his easel in the caravan that is parked in the front garden of his house and begins painting. Those milkmen and breadmen who do the early-morning shift often have cause to see the flicker of the candle through the window of the caravan as Willy works into the dawn hours.

The Candlelight Painter is an introduction to Willy Cauley's talent; it is also an introduction to an aspect of Ireland's culture of which few people are aware. The Travelling community have lived on the margins of Irish society for hundreds of years. Their culture has been much-maligned and little appreciated. This book is a small window through which we can see glimpses of this unique Irish culture, a culture with a long and proud history.

The beginning of the tóhbar (journey)

My name is William Cauley. I am a Traveller, a painter and a poet and I have now been fifty years on this earth. I was born on the twenty-third of August, 1954 in a place called Bedford Row in Limerick city. The building where I was born was next to the Savoy where there was also a hospital at one time. Life is full of coincidences and strange as it may seem I have met fifteen or sixteen people down through the years who were born in that place and on the same day as me! And I have become the best of friends with a share of those people! Isn't it a funny old world? It happened to me on a few occasions that I was drinking a pint in one of the local pubs and I struck up a conversation with another man only to find that he had been born on the exact same day as me.

I often had the same middle name in common with these men as we were all born in the Marian Year. It was a year when Irish people decided to show a special devotion to Our Lady. Many shrines and grottoes were built throughout Ireland during that year. Some of these shrines were built by the best of artists and sculptors and you can still see many of these grottoes to this day.

A Mincéir (Traveller) from day one

I inherited the Traveller musical tradition from my mother's side of the family and as far back as I can remember I was out playing music and singing on the streets of Limerick. I don't know where my painting came from but I'm sure it was in the genes somewhere back along the line.

Travellers like to travel. The Travelling people have been in Ireland a long, long time and to travel is part of our tradition and heritage. You could say that I was fond of travelling from day one. When I was only about five or six years of age I had a habit of going away down the street to play the mouth organ. And even then I didn't like to be confined to base. I liked sleeping out for the night. I would hop into a cardboard box and throw an old pullover or some old newspapers over myself to keep warm! I could be called 'Box Car Willy' to tell you the truth! As soon as the dusk fell, I'd be looking around for my bed. I'd be looking around to see what cardboard box I'd fit into.

I was born and bred in Limerick so you can say that I am Limerick through and through. I am proud of this city and yet sometimes I am ashamed by the violence of a few that tarnishes its reputation.

Mistling along the muinceara tóhbars (Travelling along the country roads)

A HOUSELESS ROAD

Four wheels a' rolling
Down a winding road
Not a house to be seen
Not a stranger in sight
The thirst for water
Lingers on and on
The horse trots slowly
Sweat from flesh and bone
A houseless road
A lonely road
The horse looks back
At a hungry man
Wondering will he stop
But on and on

He must go
For around the bend
There must be a house
A decent house
A welcoming house
With food and water
He must want.

As soon as the cuckoo called and the summer came around again my parents would move off and head for the countryside once more. We would dust off the wagon and get the horses harnessed and ready for the *tóhbar* (road). You would feel the excitement of the horses because they could sense that they would soon be free of their confinement, that they would be out in the country again. And though I loved the *helm* (city) I had a longing for the country. I longed for the wildness and freedom of it.

You see, when you are in a city, you are trapped. It is like as if you are in a cage of some sorts. And it's only when you get out into the country again that you realise this. And when we got out there in the country again we knew exactly how to survive. It was like as if we had never been away. We were surviving again from day to day, moving slowly with the wagon and the *currys* (horses) between the different country villages.

Travellers can survive anywhere, be it country or city. We are great survivors! We've had to be, I suppose! When I was in the city I knew how to play the mouth organ, to sing or to pitch pennies against the wall. I could make a few bob this way and I had a freedom of sorts. But when you got out in the country again you knew a different type of freedom, a different type of survival.

When I think back on my father now, the Lord have mercy on him, he was a great hunter. I remember well watching him hunting when I was only about four or five years of age. We would be out in the country and he would go out into a *sarc* (field), an ash plant in his *mália* (hand). He would look out across the field, his eyes scanning the high grass and he would tell me to stay still. And he would watch that blade of grass until he would see that grass breathing when the rabbit or hare came out to rest. His *oglers* (eyes) were sharp; he had great eyesight and he could see the grass breathing even from a distance. Then he would creep up to that patch of grass with his stick and we would have a rabbit for the supper! And we weren't the only ones who were having rabbit in the pot. There were many people out hunting for their dinner at that time!

They were hard times and you were glad for the bit that you got to eat. There was no such thing as grumbling or complaining about it. You were lucky to have it. You were a rich man if you had a pair of *gullimors* (shoes) then, let me tell you. It was the bare feet all year round. When you were going across the ditches to look for *chimis* (sticks) for the *glimmer* (fire), thorns from the briars would get stuck in your *cories* (feet). I remember my mother, God rest her, spending hours in the evenings next to the campfire trying to get a thorn that had gone in too deep out of some poor child's foot.

When I was small I was mad about the freedom of the countryside but it was not an easy life either. There was nothing too romantic about it. It was a tough life at the best of times. It is when I think back on it now that I realise what great-hearted people my father and mother were, the way they were able to provide for themselves and a family of sixteen children while travelling the roads. And they did all that when we, the Irish people, were amongst the poorest of the poor.

The lúbán and going to coldrom in the late molly
(The tent and sleeping in the late camp)

When we were travelling we had only two *lubáns* (tents). The girls would go in one tent and the boys in the other. And we would spread straw on the ground as our bedding. I remember how we came to a late camp in Galway one night. The *olomi* (night) had already fallen. The stars were already twinkling in the sky, that's how late we were! The camp looked perfect because it was an old *molly* (camping place). We knew it because we had been there before. Like most Travellers we liked to go back to our own camping places, the places where our family had always camped going back through the generations. Nowadays they have dumped rocks and boulders into all the old camping places. Do they know the memories of previous generations that they have buried under the rocks and the rubble? Do they care?

Anyway, we came to this place again and set up our tents in the dark. We were no sooner gone to *coldrom* (sleep) when we were getting stung! Hadn't we spread the straw on an ant hill and the ants weren't a bit happy. They were eating us so that we had lumps all over us. My poor father had to root up the tents again in the *dorchóg* (dark) and set them down the way a bit where the ants wouldn't find us. We had to leave the straw bedding where it was as it was crawling with ants. So we ended up sleeping on the damp ground that night. The *sciuch* (rain) was lashing down and the water started coming in on the ground so that our tugs (clothes) were soaked through. We were miserable with the cold and the wet that night and we didn't sleep a wink. They were tough times as compared with today. There is no doubt about that.

The slahóg and my ríb (The rat and my hair)

When you were camping you got close to nature. Nature was around you whether it be rabbits, ants, badgers or even rats! We were camping another time when I had a close encounter with a rat. I was sleeping away without a care in the world as you do when you are a child and you have no worries. And when I woke up in the morning I noticed a bit of a breeze around my head when I stepped out through the flap of the tent. My mother spotted me then and she started roaring her head off! Hadn't I lost half of my hair!

My mother thought at first that some of my older brothers had cut it off during the night for a laugh or that the fairies had got to me or something. But the real story was that a rat had been chewing away on my *ríb* (hair) during the night. He had been doing it quietly however so as not to wake me. Later that day one of my brothers discovered the rat's nest under a *claitóg* (ditch). And wasn't my hair in the nest that was under a stone wall! The rat had been making a comfortable nest for her young in the wall and she had decided to go for some luxury bedding. Strangely enough my hair is growing stronger than ever today. Many men of my age have no hair but mine is still thriving!

The Pied Piper

Rat-charming is an old skill that Travellers had in times gone by. The Pied Piper of Hamelin, the man who is mentioned in that fairytale, was a Traveller. I read somewhere that after the Second World War the Germans hired Roma Gypsy rat-charmers from Romania who played tunes and drew the rats out of all the bombed-out buildings so that the locals could build them up again in safety.

Because Travellers are good musicians they were always fond of the whistle. I heard of a Travelling man up in Donegal about ten or fifteen years ago and he would whistle and the rats would come up and play outside his caravan. There was another man who used to feed rats and of course all the neighbours were giving out about him — maybe it was the same man. He would whistle and it didn't matter what time of the day or night it was, the rats would arrive. And then they would go away when he whistled again.

There were a lot of stories in times gone by of rats saving people's lives. Talk to any of the old soldiers who are left and who were in the First World War. Men getting lost in a trench somewhere or a in a tunnel and being led to safety when all their hopes were gone. There was a case in America about twenty years ago that I heard about where an old tramp was using a scrap car as his home in some city or other. He was lonely and he used to feed the rats for company. And the car he was in went on fire one night. And whatever way things happened didn't the rats get into formation and pull him from the car before he got burnt. The cops were watching from the top of a bridge and they were sure your man was a goner as the car was like an inferno in minutes. The traces of petrol in the tank had made it burn as quick as paper.

But the tramp lived to tell the tale. He was interviewed in the newspapers and on television afterwards. He told people of how he had fed the rats over the years and how they had looked out for him in his time of need. Rats are supposed to be very intelligent animals. I know that they bit off my hair that time in the camp without even waking me–so they must be cute enough! Goldfinger! Once they didn't bite off my fingers and my toes!

Washbol and sciuch — the Mincéir way (Soap and water — the Traveller way)

I still have a full head of hair, rat or no rat! And sometimes the lads from the city here would ask me, 'Willy, how is it that your hair is all there at your age and there's not much grey in it either?' Says I to them, 'Wash your hair with two raw eggs and you'll be as sound as a bell!' That's the truth now! A raw *rumóg* (egg) does the trick. And to clean your teeth then you would have an old bit of a cloth and a bit of *lodach* (ash) out of the fire. Many settled people would have used the ash as toothpaste as well. And you were as lucky as a black cat if you owned a toothbrush. You were a millionaire if you had a toothbrush!

Getting the cure

Some of the Travellers had their own cures. Cures for boils and all the rest of it. But we would depend on the doctors too. I fell off a bridge one time when I was very young. I was messing around as you do at that age and I lost my footing. I was lucky because I nearly hurt myself seriously. As it was I got a cracked bone in my neck. So I'm in the *greechcén* (hospital) and the doctor comes over to me and he says, 'Would you like a horse?' I says to him, 'Are you giving him to me for nothing?' And he replies, 'Oh, I have him below in the field there — you can have him,' he says. 'There's only one condition,' he says. 'You can have him providing you take that medicine there.' He was bribing me, of course! I was only four or five at the time, and of course, I fell for the bribe! I'm still waiting for that horse — Doctor, you better watch out!

When I was in the hospital my father came in one day to visit me on his own *curry* (horse). We were on the road at the time and my family were staying a good few miles outside the city so he had a bit of a journey to the hospital. So he came into the hospital and I was let out. I packed the few clothes I had and I tied them in a *lampo* (bag) around my waist. So he lifts me up on the horse and hops up behind me himself. What happened but didn't I lose my balance and fall off the horse, and the two of us at the entrance to the hospital! And my father whispers to me, 'Are you ever going to learn to stand up or sit up or something?' I had strained my neck a bit again but there was no way I was going back into the hospital. The smell of the horse and the fresh air were enough for me. We galloped out of there, the two of us riding bareback.

I have always loved horses and none of us liked saddles on horses that time either. If you had a saddle on your horse you were like one of the lords — one of the gentry! One of those English fellas with the tweeds!

Limerick city is a lot different now. I see my own sons and they can't keep horses anymore. The city life — it changes everything. Who knows what else will change in the next few years? Wouldn't you love to able to see into the future for just a few quick minutes? A quick peek! Will we see the Travelling man wearing glasses? Isn't it true? You would very seldom see a Travelling person wearing glasses. But they probably will eventually — what's the bets? They will probably admit that they need them and give into them eventually. As long as they don't go around with umbrellas over their heads! Now that would be something! Did you ever see a Travelling man with an umbrella?

A busy gália (child)

I was the second oldest in my family. I had a sister who was older than me but strangely enough I used to do most of the babysitting of my younger brothers and sisters myself. My sister was a bit of a rambler and she would be off rambling around the city with our cousins. This meant that yours truly was left with the babysitting. I was a busy *gália* (child), getting the water, getting the sticks, putting down the old breakfast. Sometimes my father and mother would be gone off to the country in the horse and cart looking for work so that we could have our next meal. So I would be left holding the fort at home until they came back. My father worked as a chimney sweep and as a tinsmith to make money. My mother made money through ballad singing or hawking swag. She would sell old clothes when they called to someone's *rodas* (door) or sometimes she would beg some *rabhta* (milk), some *fé* (meat) or some *lúrp* (flour).

My mother was well-known in Limerick as one of the best of the old-time ballad-singers. You could say that both my father and mother made music so as to provide themselves with a living. He would be in the yard beating his rhythms on the tin, mending the buckets and the gallons and she might be in the kitchen singing songs from the ballad sheets. I learnt a lot of the old songs from her and it was when we called to the farmers' houses that I learnt them. She would tell them what ballad sheets she had for sale and they would request a particular ballad. They would buy the ballad sheet from her and then she would sing the ballad that they had just bought. Sometimes the farmers couldn't read and they would just pick a sheet that they liked the look of. It could have been any song but she would sing the ballad for them anyway. My mother was well-read and she could read the ballad sheets but she didn't have to. All the ballads were in her head since time immemorial. She had heard different versions of them for years, listening to her relations sitting around the fire. Often the whole farmer's family would gather around to listen to her voice.

She might have two hundred ballad sheets in her basket as we went from door to door in the city or farm to farm in the country. People didn't have so many radios that time and they were dying to hear a song. It was better than the Top Thirty! She might get half a crown for a ballad sheet and a song.

My gathrum and my nadherum (My father and mother)

My father's name was Michael Cauley and he was a West of Ireland Traveller. He was actually born in Roscommon. Generations of Cauleys came from the west and they were originally from counties like Sligo, Mayo and Roscommon. They were like a lot of Travelling people in this sense. If you look at families like the Wards, the McDonaghs and the Mongans—most of them came from the West of Ireland originally. Certain Travelling families came from certain regions in Ireland and no matter where they travelled during the course of their lives, they would often go back to those places to be buried.

My wife's people are McCarthys. They are from the south, from counties like Cork and Limerick. The Delaneys would be from the south-east, from counties like Carlow and Kilkenny. The Cashes, Connors' and Berrys would be from the south-east also, from counties like Wexford and Wicklow. Up north then you had the McGinleys, the Dohertys and the O'Rourkes.

My mother's maiden name was Julie McCarthy. Her family were

nearly all reared in Limerick city. Her family used to live at one time in a large house near the Limerick market known as the Mill House. The Mill House was a huge house with about ten or fifteen rooms in it and different families would live in the different rooms. My mother's people used to use the Mill House as a base during the winter but they would leave it to go travelling during the summer months. Her family worked at the same trades as most other Travellers. The men cleaned chimneys and mended buckets and farm tools. The women sold swag from house to house, sold ballad sheets and told fortunes sometimes and they made and sold their own paper flowers.

I don't know where my father and mother met the first day ever. I'm not sure when the romance struck! I never really found out about that because they never really told us. There was a tension between them because they had different outlooks on life. My father was the kind of Traveller who wanted the freedom of the open road. He was happy just to get his chimney sticks and head for the open *tóhbar* (road). My mother was different — she preferred the city. She had been reared in the city and she preferred that we children stay in the city so that we could have a regular education. My mother was a very educated person. She loved reading the newspapers whenever she could get her hands on them. And I think it was her who instilled a fondness for words in me also. I think she was my first inspiration for writing poetry. She had worked in Cleeves factory, in Limerick city when she was growing up. She was very fond of reading and you could say that she was more of an urban person than my father who preferred camping and the country life. So there was a tension there that couldn't easily be resolved.

We camped around the city for years but by the time we actually moved into a *cén* (house) in 1970 my father was never going to adapt to the settled life. He would be gone out into the country, out to do his tinwork and chimney-work in the rural villages like Cappamore and Murroe and he would only come back when night fell. He was very browned off with the house and with city life. He would never have been able to get used to it. That first house that we moved into was in a place called O'Malley Park in Southill. It had a name for roughness in later years but it was a peaceful place when it was first built. We were one of the first Traveller families to be housed in that estate.

Mistling in the munia weather (Travelling in the good weather)

TO HEAR AND TO SEE

To listen to the early bird
singing a new day new
like the first day of life
God's power and might
to listen to the whispering breeze
fluttering the autumn leaves
to see the sun's rays beaming
from a powerful sky
or the dewdrops falling
from the morning light
to hear the cuckoo
on a bright summer's day
or see a flower a'blooming
in the merry month of May
to see the moon glowing
from the cloudless sky
and the wind softly blowing
brings all a new joy.

The happiest moment for me as a young Traveller was when the summer days arrived. That was the happiest time because you could run across the fields and be free. You were free like a bird, like the rabbits in the field, you could run and be free. In summer you could camp out and sleep without a *ráiblín* (blanket) when the weather was warmest. I used to love running through the meadows especially if the grass was long. Sometimes you would disturb a hare where it lay sleeping somewhere and it would burst out in front of you, the grass still warm where it had been resting.

I remember my father and myself working at the hay with the farmers. I would be helping them fork the hay and stack it. We would shake it out on the forks and you would see the *bini slahógs* (tiny field-mice) running away where we had disturbed their nests. After a few hours I would skip away for a break. I would have a drink of lemonade hidden in a cool place under a *caideóg* (rock) or near a stream and I would grab a bundle of hay and go out to a part of the field where the hay hadn't been cut yet. Sometimes I got so comfortable that I fell asleep and awoke to the sound of the men looking for me!

Mistling (travelling) with the family

I remember those days of camping like they were only yesterday. I have a good memory for things that happened when I was very young — say four or five years of age. When you were camping you'd only get up very early if you were bored or the weather outside was very warm, a lovely fresh morning. Either that or you were hungry and you could see the pot abroad on the fire and that your mother and father were still asleep. And you wanted to get in there first for the grub!

Myself and my mother would often get the fire going first. I would get the sticks and she would arrange them That was the first job on every campsite. Get the pot and the *sriteal* (kettle) down. After that my father would have an old *steemer* (cigarette) and then we would head off into the countryside with the chimney sticks and the toolbag with his mending gear for mending buckets. We would be gone for four, five or maybe six hours at a time. Then we might come back and have a sup of tae at the fire. Then I would often head off with my mother for some more hard walking. We would go a different road to the one my father had travelled for another couple of hours and my mother would be hawking the holy pictures, the ballad sheets and the paper flowers. We often camped near a crossroads because then we could change direction more easily depending on how trade was going. So we would try out one *tóhbar* (road) first. Then the next day we would try out another road, the day after another one again; different routes.

The pattern on the tóhbar (road)

Another reason we were fond of the crossroads was the pattern. When we Travellers travelled in a big group together, say two sets of families, one family would be gone on a few miles ahead of the other. And when they came to a crossroads they might take a left turn. But to remind the people behind they would pick out some sods of grass and make a special sign on the wall or on the side of the road. This sign was sometimes known as a pattern. It has died out now with the big highways we have cutting through the countryside.

A bini stafara (A small prayer) 'God bless this house and all that's in it'

My father was a lover of nature and the countryside and he liked the country so much that he sometimes avoided the roads altogether. When we were out tinsmithing or chimney-sweeping he would often walk through the fields instead of going along the road. If he saw a house over in the distance there he would make a beeline for it. He was a really focused kind of a fella, always focused on the next job. And he would climb over walls, go over ditches and gates and whatever. And I'd be following behind him, running to catch up with him because he was a great walker. And he'd drag me through ditches and thorns and the thorns would be stuck to my legs.

When my father called to a house, the first thing he would say would be 'God bless the house'. If he saw another workman there he would say 'God bless the work'. If there were people at home you were bound to get a couple of jobs anyway. They would ask you to clean the *chimbley* (chimney) and then you were going to mend a bucket or some pot that had a hole in it, because a tinsmith mightn't have visited them for months. And they might have some old damaged buckets lying there but they didn't want to have to go away and buy a new bucket. All it would take my father was *ód niucs* (two pennies). He would put one in the top and one in the bottom of the bucket and splice the bucket back together again and the job was done.

What he used to do as well was he would make his own pannies — little milk cans — he would have a load of them hanging from his back as we walked along. Little churns — he would make them, and aluminium cups too. That's what we used to use for our own meals back at the camp. We used to have an aluminium plate that he was after making himself, an aluminium spoon, an aluminium cup! Everything was all aluminium! Strange, isn't it?

My nadherum — the beor with the munia greesh (My mother — the woman with the big heart)

I was very close to my mother when I was growing up. I was her favourite in a sense although I was only the second eldest in my family. When I was small she used to make me tag along behind her when she was working. She could be selling swag at the houses or washing clothes or organising the other children or the campfire. It made no difference what she was working at because she would always be singing. And I would be learning the tunes at the same time. I would sing them and whistle them. I loved whistling so much that there were very few birds in the trees that I couldn't imitate. The robin, the blackbird, the thrush — I could whistle back to them like I was one of their own! Maybe I confused the poor creatures! I was mad about music and singing because my mother was mad about them too.

My mother often sang just for the fun when we all sat around the campfire in the evening. She would be boiling a pot and singing away, getting the 'late supper' as they called it, ready for a gang of hungry mouths! Her singing helped her stay happy. She was always a happy person despite the conditions we faced, especially during winter — the children coming out of the tents with no shoes, walking on the damp and freezing ground in their bare feet.

Someday I will try and capture this misery in a painting. I will get a huge canvas, the biggest one I can find, and when the painting is done I will show it to the press and the government so as to make a statement to them. 'Look at it, this is how the government ignored us back through time. This is how you hurt these people's minds then, a hurt that later changed into a depression. At a later stage you forced them into houses. You blocked up their roads.' I will put all my energies into that painting. Everything.

Mixing with other Mincéir (Travellers)

We usually travelled in a family group. My father, my mother and the children. That was it. It was easier to get work if we didn't travel in very large groups. There was only so much work going in every country village. Sometimes we would meet other Travellers along the way. If we knew the family very well we might camp beside them for the night.

The odd time we might even stay camped with another family for a week or so before we would all up and go our separate ways. Sometimes the men might go on an old drinking spree, especially if they hadn't seen some of their relations or friends for a long time. That *dorchóg* (night) us children would be gone to *luí* (bed) but we wanted to be part of the excitement and find out what the news was — who was getting married, who was gone to England, who had fallen out with who.

And we waited for them in the *half-lodas* (half-light) that was the inside of the *lúbán* (tent) waiting for the men to come home. As soon as we thought we could hear their voices we would come out of the tents and boil up some *sciuch-elpi* (boiling water) so as to have a *dreep of weed* (cup of tea) ready for them when they came back to the *molly* (camp). You could hear them from miles away when you were out the countryside because the countryside is so quiet at night. You would hear them singing and the *comras* (dogs) barking in the farmer's house and we'd say, 'They're coming back'. I'd be there sitting with the rest of the family at the *glimmer* (fire). Once I'd hear the dogs barking in the darkness I'd say, 'Lads they're coming along the road! Any minute, they'll be here. They'll be singing or killing each other or both!'

Getting *lósped (married)*

Certain families liked to make matches between the young people in times past. You can see it if you were to start doing the family trees of different Traveller families. We Travellers tended to marry Travellers from neighbouring counties, people that we knew distantly or had some connection with in some way. In that way all the families in a certain area would be married in through one another and they could support each other better through times of trouble or hardship.

Many of the settled people had matchmakers in their communities. That was a man who would try to match people who he thought would get on well together and whose families would suit one another from the point of view of passing on the land to the next generation. The Travellers didn't have so many matchmakers that I heard of, although there was a man called Cowboy McDonagh about fifty years ago who made matches for many of the Travellers in Galway.

When I was growing up the older people would often make a joke or a half-joke when they were talking about children, 'When my Jimmy is older he'll marry your Bridie', and all the rest of it. Sometimes it might happen that things turned out that way but more often than not it didn't. Certain families preferred matchmaking but that system didn't work for everybody.

I'm fifty years of age now myself and I know that even within my own family and generation the matchmaking was never such a big thing. Who we got married to was entirely our free choice. It was boy meet girl and then there was love. It was up to ourselves when my wife and I got married. We knew each other from way back, from when we were children. We grew up together here in Limerick city and the truth is that we both knew too much about each other! My wife's maiden name was Bridget McCarthy. At that time the McCarthy Travellers in Limerick city tended to marry into other McCarthys or Cauleys. There was a connection there somewhere along the line. The McDonaghs were another Travelling family that the Cauleys would have married into. There are Travellers known as Cauley all over Ireland. I know that there are many Cauleys in Dublin who have been there for years. There are also Cauleys in Thurles, County Tipperary and in England too. The person who draws up the family tree would have some job, connecting everybody up together!

Our dhíls scurlimed (Burning us out)

We passed through many different *helms* (towns) on our travels and although we tended to stay in the south of the country we sometimes travelled up towards Galway and the west of Ireland too. We always found that the more familiar the settled people were with you, the more friendly they were towards you. The people out around Newport and East Limerick were generally very friendly to us, because they knew our family going back through the generations. If we went to somewhere where we were strangers, things could be difficult. I will never forget what happened near Oranmore when I was only four years old.

We had no wagon at that time and we were camped in our *lúbáns* in against the side of a ditch. You were one of the better-off Travelling families if you had your own wagon at that time. My mother had been walking from house to house that day selling mothballs and holy pictures and when we made camp for the night my father left the horse into some farmer's field without asking permission. He should not have done that, of course, but the next thing we knew there were shouts outside our tents and we came out in the darkness to find a bunch of angry farmers standing around the camp with huge torches that were on fire. They told us to get out of the area or they would burn us out.

I remember being very *geitilt* (frightened). When you are a child and you are standing there in the darkness and all these angry faces around you roaring and shouting . . . It was like a scene from one of those films you see about the Ku Klux Klan and the way that they used to attack the black people in America in times gone by. We all had to pack up there and then and go away even though it was the black of night.

That was my one bad memory of Oranmore and naturally enough we never camped there again. Before that I had always enjoyed visiting the place because there was a convent there where the nuns were very nice. They were mad about me because I used to sing to them and anytime I called there they would give me a big meal and then give me a rake of food to bring back to my family. They were nice, kindhearted people, those nuns in Oranmore.

Resting in the old céns (houses)

We never took lodgings in settled people's houses like Travellers might have done years before us. We might stay in an old house that was condemned, maybe an old lodge that was on the way into a mansion, a derelict lodge house. We would put the whole lot in, camp, tent, straw, put the donkey out the back, and light our fire somewhere. And stay in there just overnight. You wouldn't stay there for a couple of days. You would be on the move again because you needed food, you would have to go and find grub. If it was a very bad winter's night we'd have to go into one of those condemned houses. We would have stayed in hay sheds sometimes, too, when the weather was very bad. Some farmers would have pity on you. Or some might just give you a big load of hay for your tent. Some farmers were very decent like that. They wouldn't leave you short a bit of hay for the tent or for feed for the horses.

Talking of the lodge houses there, we came across the old gentry once or twice. We came across one English fella up in Tipperary somewhere. This fella was very strict altogether. He didn't want us anywhere near his property at all. I was surprised because the fella had so much land; it would have been no skin off his nose to let us in to one of the fields for the night. The local sergeant came up and he said, 'Lads, I'm not against ye at all.' He was an old man, this sergeant, and he said, 'It's not my fault — but he wants ye to move.' This is a good few years back now. And I said to him, 'C'mere, Sergeant. There he is now, an English lord in our land, our nation.' And the sergeant understood. He had great pity, great respect. And he said, 'Listen, try and stay one night and I'll do my best to get around him. I'll say that there's someone sick or something.' So he got around your man anyway and we were able to stay the night.

As we were passing out of the lord's land the next day, we passed right by the front of his mansion. It was the finest of houses with a big driveway leading up to it and we started to take the mickey. 'Oh ho, tallyho old chap.' We could see your man inside watching us through a window, a stern look on his face. And he had a hat with the feather hanging out of it. We were having a good laugh over it as we went out on the main road again. 'I'd say he's going off foxhunting now, I'd say old chap. Really! Oxford, Cambridge!'

We never travelled too far away from the Limerick area. No matter where we went we always circled back towards Limerick. My mother always wanted to come back—she would get lonesome for her own people. There was a drawback there, a drawback towards Limerick. But my father for his part used to get depressed coming back into the city.

The tóm lúbán and the bini lúbán (The big tent and the little tent)

When I was young very few Travellers had motorised caravans. Maybe a few families in Dublin did but even there they were fairly scarce. The most that Travellers had were horse-drawn wagons and camps. You could make two types of tent then depending on the situation. A small tent was quick enough to make. You would get some wattles together. Hazel were the best as they were easier to bend, and when you bent them they stayed bent. The best thing to do was to cut the hazel fresh from the trees. You would carve them then, pare the ends of them off and sharpen the ends so that they could stick into the ground. A good trick was to light a fire under them then so that you would heat them up and make them flexible. So when you got ready to spread your canvas out over the tent, the rib cage would already be bent into shape for you.

We used a tent called a shelter-tent very often too. This was a big tent which had a smaller tent attached to one end of it. It was a tent-version of those igloos the Eskimos have in the North Pole. In the old-style shelter camp you could stand in one section of the tent and bend down to move into the other section which was where you went to sleep. The whole tent was made out of wattles which you bent over to form a round shape; then you attached canvas sacks as a cover. Some other thinner wattles were attached to a runner going from the big tent to the smaller tent. It was a skill in itself to put up a shelter tent correctly. It was another skill again to take it all down again when you were being chased away by the locals in the middle of the night!

The girls would sleep in one section and the boys in another. One bad thing about a shelter tent was that you were blinded with smoke as it wasn't so easy for the smoke to escape. Eventually you got used to the smoke. You were born into it. There was a small place in the middle-top of the tent for the smoke to escape but all the smoke wouldn't escape away through that unfortunately. A draught or a breeze coming in would send the smoke every-which-way because the fire was in the middle of the tent.

Despite the stinging smoke I always preferred to sleep in a tent. Even when we got our own wagon I still felt safer in the tent, believe it or not. It could be dangerous enough in stormy weather if you were inside in a horse-drawn wagon. The wagon was perched high up on the wheels and it could easily fall over in the wind. You would hear stories of Travelling people who would go to sleep in their tents for the night and wake up the next morning to find their wagon a hundred yards away down the road. The wagon might just have rolled out off the grass bank with the strength of the wind. I remember a man named Jim Reilly whose wagon moved away off and up into the middle of the road on him while he was asleep. Luckily for him, cars were fairly scarce on the Irish roads back then. It couldn't happen today.

Another dangerous thing in stormy weather for the wagon-owner was fire. There was a small stove in every wagon to keep people warm. Travellers would very seldom quench their stoves at night and the timber inside a wagon was very dry. If the wagon tilted over then in a storm it could easily go on fire and you could be trapped inside the wagons with the flames.

Corribed with the crolus (Starved with the hunger)

You always had to be careful of the *stémons* (rats) when you were setting up the tents. Rats can be dangerous especially if they are cornered. They are also very dangerous if they get near children or babies because they carry a disease called Weil's disease which can cause death. I remember a Travelling man named Reilly who was from County Monaghan originally and he was camping in a tent near our family one night when a rat ran up his clothes. He had a hold of him inside the leg of his pants so that the rat couldn't bite him and the poor man came out of his tent roaring with fright. The poor man had to take off his pants in the middle of the road so that he could get rid of the rat.

When you put down a tent at the side of the ditch you always had to make sure that the tent was well away from a rat's burrow. Rats have a certain 'run', a certain path that they always follow. If you put down a tent that blocked the path to their lair it would make no difference to them. They would just eat their way through the tent so that they could keep following their run and God help you if you were in the way!

At that time most Travelling families like us had a timber box with a hinge on it called a grub-box where we could store our food in safety. It was a big strong box so that neither damp nor animals could do damage to it and it was kept in the wagon when we were on the road. The hinge was to keep the rats and mice out. There was also a lock and key to go with many grub-boxes too! That was to stop the greedy fella who would get up during the night and take half of the food while everybody else was snoring!

When my mother was young and living in the Mill House in Limerick city a relative of mine had the key to the grub-box. She was in charge of it. And what did one of her brothers who was hungry do one night but go around into the next room and bore a hole through the wall and right into this grub-box which was leaning against the wall! He was a real James Bond let me tell you! So he got a whole pile of food and stuffed himself to the gills. And his poor sister was the one who got the blame as nobody owned up to it. Wasn't he an awful man too? They were hungry times. It's hard to believe it now and it was only a few short years ago too when you think about it. There are so many people in Ireland now who could buy a thousand grub-boxes and fill them and still have money left over to spend!

I remember another Travelling man whose family were travelling with us back near Ennistymon in County Clare a good few years back. He was sitting at the campfire *corribed* with the *crolus* (starved with the hunger). And his wife came back from *géigin'* the *helm* (begging in the town). And her husband was sitting there impatiently and the pot of water boiling, waiting for her. And he says to his wife when he first spotted her coming up the road to the camp, 'Will you come in before my belly hits my backbone? Will you come on will you? Look, the pot is boiled and steamin,' he says. And she opened up her shawl and took out some *pek* (food) that she had got from the local people. He got the cabbage, the spuds and the skins and threw the whole lot into the water. Now did you ever see a fella boiling cabbage and spuds at the one time, and the spuds with the skins still on them! And he had an old bit of a stick and he was beatin' it into the spuds and he saying, 'Come on, boil up will ye, boil, boil, boil, boil!' And he beatin' the stick into the pot! He was the strangest man I ever saw in my life! The poor man had gone temporarily around the bend with the hunger!

Goats were a great source of vitamins for us back then. Goats are tough animals who don't need too much care. They aren't fussy and they can survive on the roughest and poorest of ground. They also eat a lot of herbs which means their *alamach* (milk) is rich in vitamins. Back then Travellers would give this milk to their children to drink and it was great for preventing chest problems and bronchitis which some families suffered badly from because of the damp conditions they were living in. And the adults would take a sup of the milk themselves also, in their *weed* (tea). You could get a pint and a half of milk from a goat in a day and that's the truth.

The Limerick umbrella-fixers

There were Travelling men who were experts at fixing umbrellas at one time too. I remember a lovely man named John-Joe Criggs. He died about twenty years ago, may he rest in peace. He was a Travelling man from Limerick who got a house eventually in Kileely, in Limerick city where he decided to settle down for the rest of his days. He used to go around the outskirts of Limerick city and all over the inner-city and he would get young fellas to collect little bits of copper wire for him. And he would fix broken umbrellas, a trade for which there was a big demand one time. God knows umbrellas are always needed in this country seeing as we get the odd drop of rain! Umbrella-fixing was John-Joe Criggs' gift, his own trade.

He didn't go around with a horse and cart. He walked instead and he was well-known all over Limerick city. He was famed all over whether it be in Raheen, in Corbally, in Castletroy. He was a grand old man to talk to and people would often give him a sup of tea as he was going about his work. His family of Travellers, the Criggs, were married into Travelling people known as the Kielys.

It's very seldom nowadays that you will see a Travelling person by themselves. It is kind of changed now. In the old days there would have been a lot of Travellers travelling by themselves. In a sense you get more that way. You get more in houses, you get more work. When you are with company, you have to share more. If there are three families together everything has to be divided up and shared between a bigger group of people. Two fellas can't mend one bucket! You can't be putting two brushes up the one chimney! One sweeper!

It was very seldom that we would have stayed in a big group together in the old days. The exception would have been if we were getting together to celebrate a wedding or a christening. We might all go on a drinking spree then with all of our relatives, including those people we hadn't seen for a while. Another time that we used to get together in a big group was when we were going on holidays—say down to Ballybunion or some other County Kerry town where there were blue skies and golden sand.

But we would never stay too long together. It might be a week. A fortnight at the most. We'd get itchy feet and head off again. The next time we might meet our cousins would be when we came around a corner with the horse and wagon and there they were! It might be time for another spree. Spree is a word that I love. It's a great word and it comes from the Irish word *'spraoí'*. Like a lot of our words in the Traveller language, Gammon, you can't do justice to it when you translate it. It means so many things all at once. Joy, happiness, fun, having the craic!

Calling to the céns (houses)

My mother always had her 'regular' houses where she would call to sell her bits and pieces or *géig* (beg) a few potatoes or some milk or some tea. She knew the women in these houses well and they always treated her well. She would be invited into the house and herself and the woman of the house would sit down and have a cup of tea and a chat. But my mother was never afraid to call into any house that she passed, whether they were regulars or not. She wouldn't be *aneishif* (ashamed) because she knew that she had to look after her family.

When us kids got a bit older things got a little bit easier because the government gave everybody a little bit through the dole. My father was always working too. He was a hard worker and he knew a lot of people out in the country areas and he always did different jobs for them. He was very fond of country people. There was no roguery about the man. He was straightforward. He would go into a house and say 'God bless the house, God bless the work' and he would do an honest job also. He was honest and straightforward and he was respected by people for that. There was no slyness about him. He was not trying to catch people

out. When he went out to a pub he would mix with anyone. He treated
everyone as an equal.

Going to school

When I got my first mouth organ the first tune that I learnt was *Silent
Night* and I was very young at the time. I was determined to learn
anything I could at the time because my education was on and off,
moving from one camp site to another. So I did not get the full education
that my mind needed. Man is nothing without knowledge. I was slow
but willing.

I might get a month here in Connemara — I might get another month
down in Kerry. Sure I might get two weeks in Newport in Tipperary.
That's the way it was in my time. Of course it wasn't easy because what
I was after learning in the last school was gone out of me — and now I
was gone into a different thing. I can read and write now — perfect. It
was very difficult back then. And every time you came into a school you
were a stranger to the locals. You were an outsider because you were
not from down the road and all the rest of it.

Most of the settled lads were spotless. They had better clothes and
they had shoes when you had none. So you stood out a bit. You could
see them looking over at you and thinking to themselves, 'Jaysus, that
fella is going to have to get an old bath soon!'

I liked English at school. That was one of my favourite subjects. I liked
words and the sounds of them. But what I liked most were the teachers
when they drew things on the blackboard. The strange writing and
shapes that they did with the chalk, the coloured chalk especially. I used
to always love the colours. It was an inspiration to me then and became
more so when I thought about it as I got older.

The subject that I didn't like was maths. I found that subject unnatural. The only people who like maths, I think, are people who love making money — the fellas who are going to make a fortune. But a fella like myself who had no future and no money ahead of him. What's the point of him adding and subtracting?

First Communion and Confirmation

I made both my Holy Communion and my Confirmation in Limerick city. People say that the Communion Day is all to do with money today — children seeing how many euro they received. We had the custom of money-giving in my time too but it was mainly pennies that you collected! I was prepared for Holy Communion in a school over near Saint John's parish. The nuns prepared me. When Travellers were on the road they would make sure that for their children to come back to the city to make their Holy Communion and Confirmation. It was the custom for a lot of us Traveller lads to leave school after we made our Holy Communion — or in a few cases, after we had made our Confirmation — and if you didn't like the chalkdust and the books you were looking forward no end to the day of your Holy Communion.

Life is changing now. Some Travellers, both boys and girls, stay on in school until their Confirmation or beyond. My own two daughters, Lily and Rosie, have stayed on at Secondary School for a good few years after their Confirmation and I am hoping that they stay on in school as long as possible. They are two very educated girls at this stage and I am hopeful that there is something good ahead of them in their lives. I think in my heart and soul that there is something more there for them ahead. There has to be. I mean what is the idea of all this education if there is nothing there for them in the future? What was it all for? What I would love to see happening in the future is that my own children would go for a job — to become secretaries or the like — and that they would make a go of things and become successful in life.

My nadherum and the lubas (My mother and words)

My mother loved reading. She would read newspapers and she loved *Ireland's Own*. She would read whenever she got a chance. She was always very keen on education. I think the main reason she was interested in it was because she had a good education herself. She could pick up a newspaper and read it which was beautiful too. She had more of a settled life in Limerick city. She didn't do much travelling.

I think it was my mother got me interested in poetry and writing the first day ever. She would read aloud to me sometimes and it was through her singing and reading that I learned a love of sounds. The sounds and rhythms of words — they make a language of their own just like painting. I wrote poetry about fifteen years ago and I had it published in newspapers and magazines. The *Limerick Leader* published my poems regularly. Today I concentrate almost entirely on painting. That takes up all of my energies but who knows? I might go back again to the poetry one of these days.

I hope that you, the reader, enjoy the poems which I have written in this book. They come from my heart. I can't say anything else about them. The poem 'Old Rosie' is about an old woman sleeping rough the streets. One night the cold is too much for her and her soul says it has had enough and flies away to Heaven.

The cold and perishing wind blows up through the street.
Old Rosie strolls down with weak and blistering feet,
No place to shelter, no place to sleep,
Maybe in the park on some old seat.
Poor Rosie, no friends to meet
And only stray dogs for friends.
And now as the darkness drifts slowly in,
This homeless woman dies on the street.

It's a lonesome, sad poem but it represents a truth, because this is what happened to one old woman in Limerick city a good few years back. Her name was Rosie and she used to sleep out, hail or shine. She slept in the doorways and searched for food from the dustbins. And she always had the stray dogs for friends.

I recited that poem on a poetry programme on Clare FM once in the company of the poet Maureen Sparling. She lives down in King's Island; she's a great poet and she has written many books. And she mentioned me in two of her books. She wrote poems about me. and she said to me, 'The next time I write about you, Willy, is when you are gone up to Heaven.' And I replied, 'Let's hope I get there first, then I'll be happy!'

Maureen Sparling's husband died a while back and he was a lovely man too. Like a lot of nice people he was mad about nature. The back of his house was full of nature. He had chickens and goats, feathers everywhere! He reminded me of some of the older Travellers in days gone by who used to have pet birds in cages, hanging from the sides of their wagons, the colours of the birds' feathers melting into the lovely decorations of the wagons. I would love to have had the budgies and the parrots when I was a young fella but we never had them. We barely fed ourselves at that time never mind the birds! We were lucky to have the dogs to watch out for us!

The gálias (children)

My father and mother died quite a few years ago, may they rest in peace. My father was only forty-five years of age when he died, may he rest in peace. He committed suicide, God rest him. He was suffering from a deep depression and he was suffering badly. I don't know how my mother managed then but I suppose she had no choice. She had to manage and get by somehow. I think city life was at the root of a lot of his depression. His generation of Travellers had seen their world turned upside-down. The traditional trades were starting to die out and so Travellers had no choice but to move into the cities to seek work. The tin-smithing died with the arrival of the factory-produced buckets and the farm work that Travellers did at the harvests disappeared with the arrival of farm machinery.

The city life really got to my father. He liked the old Traveller life, travelling through the rural villages and working for the country people. He became depressed as his life changed with the dying out of the chimney-sweeping and the tinwork. Like many other Travellers he became depressed with being cooped up in the city and stuck in a house all day. While my mother was a very sociable person my father was a different personality. He was more of a loner. I suppose you could say he was kind of lonely in his mind. Even though he was married and he eventually settled down in a house there was just something missing in his life. The minute that we would come into Limerick in the horse-drawn caravan he would get this lonesome fit and he was mad to go back out to the country again. He got so depressed one time that he cut off two of his fingers with a hatchet. That was how depressed he was.

In the years since he died I often wondered about his life and I believe now it was the city life that caused him so much anguish. I think all Travellers have been affected by the change to city life in one way or another. You hear of older Travelling people even today and they get very depressed because of the changes that have happened in their lives. They are often squashed in on some site somewhere without the freedom to travel anymore. In the old days they could have pulled their caravan into the side of a ditch. They could have watched the autumn leaves, the robin whistling near the campfire or listened to the first cuckoo in summertime. That life is all gone now and that peace of mind is gone. Now the mind is all confusion. It is like a big trap and it is very sad.

Trapped by the helm (city) life

When I think of my father—sure he had been on the move since the day he was born! It is no wonder that the sight of the city or of any large town was enough to get him down. Once he saw the open sky and the fields he became a new man. I wonder how many older Travellers became depressed because they weren't allowed to travel anymore? How many of them became depressed when they saw their traditional camping places being blocked up and they ended up drifting from the countryside into houses and the cities?

I have eight brothers and sisters who are still living and this is out of a family of fourteen children. Less than half of us are still on this earth. Eight of us have now passed on, a bed in Heaven to them. Our family had a lot of tragedy. Mary-Bridget, Joseph, Eddie, Thomas and Julia all died when they were only young and in their prime. Julia and Eddie died across the water in England as they had emigrated there to look for a better life. A number of my brothers and sisters who are now dead suffered from depression while they were alive. I think the city life may have had a lot to do with it. Freedom and travelling were in their blood and being cooped up in the city affected them and made them sick. So there was a lot of tragedy in my family going back along the way. It was tough and very, very sad.

I often used to feel very down about the fact that our lives were so hard and I missed my brothers and sisters who had died when they were only in their prime. Sometimes I don't know how I managed to pull through myself with all that suffering around me. It was tough, that's for sure. There are eight of us still alive, thank God. There are my sisters Margaret, Noreen, Winifred and Nan; and my brothers Mikey, Stephen, Patrick and John.

Travelling across the sciuch (water)

Unusually enough for a Travelling family, there is only one of my sisters in England now. My sister Noreen is over across the water. She is married and settled down over there. Funnily enough, nearly all the members of my family who went to England married settled people over there whereas nearly all of my brothers and sisters who stayed in Ireland married Travellers. England is a bigger country and there isn't the same kind of prejudice over there from everybody. My youngest brother Eddie is a good example. He was going out with a settled English girl before he died. He was a landscape gardener just outside London and was doing very well for himself. Then he died tragically in an accident. It was the saddest thing ever. He was a great worker and had his own business cards printed out. This girl used to come back here regularly to visit his grave. And she would always bring flowers to lay on his grave. The two of them had been madly in love before he died so tragically in an accident. It was so sad to see their love destroyed by such tragedy. Life can be a hard road.

The sublias and the laicíns (The other boys and girls in the family)

Most of my brothers and sisters who are in Ireland are still living in the Munster region. Michael, Stephen, Patrick all live in the Limerick area like myself. I live in the city, my brother Patrick lives in Cappamore, a village in East Limerick. My brother Stephen bought his own house in Ennis, County Clare and another brother Mikey also lives in Clare.

I have a brother John who's over in England somewhere but I haven't heard from him in a while. He travels around a bit so he could be anywhere right now. He sends the odd letter but I haven't received one in a while. So if you read this book, John, make sure and get in touch! John is a good worker and he works with his hands. He is a good gardener and sometimes he works as a labourer also. He is married to a Travelling girl and they are a very close couple. In other words you don't see one without the other! They are like John Wayne now and Maureen O'Hara in that film *The Quiet Man*.

All my brothers and sisters who live in Ireland are married into Travelling families, just like myself. Pat is married to a McCarthy, a woman named Constance McCarthy. Mikey is married to one of the McDonaghs from Ennis, Anne McDonagh. My sister Marguerita's man is one of the Caseys from Limerick city who are also a Travelling family. It is very interesting to see all the connections between different families through all the different *lóspos* (marriages). Someday someone should do the family tree so that all the family relationships and connections can be traced.

'The times they are a-changing'

It was the singer Bob Dylan who said those words and wasn't he right too? Things are changing very fast in Irish people's lives now. There was a time not so long ago when the extended family was very important whether you were a settled person or a Traveller. But that is changing now. I would say the family and the support of the family is more important still in the Travelling community than it is in the settled community, but even amongst Travellers things are changing very quickly. There was a time when everybody in the family would stick together very closely to survive. Now it's becoming more individual. What happens a lot now is that when the parents of a large family die the whole family splits and everybody becomes a little unit by himself. People don't stick together as much anymore.

I was watching a programme on television one night recently that put me in mind of the way things are changing. It was about three brothers who were living the old family way. They were farmers from a rural part of Mayo, three lone brothers all living in the same house. They were only in their late fifties but the great thing about them was they stuck together. The three of them were looking out for one another. One brother did the cooking. Another brother went to the local town to get whatever they needed. A third brother made all their clothes. He was a weaver and he would weave pullovers, blankets and any other clothes they needed. They prayed together before every meal and the most beautiful thing about them was that they would kneel down every evening and say the rosary together before they went to bed. It was obvious from the programme that they were very happy and loyal to one another. And with the help of God there is a *luí* (bed) in Heaven for them because they deserve it. Fellas like them are a dying breed. You would never really get that class of people in Ireland anymore.

The lone boys

When I was young there used to be a lot of stories about the 'lone boys' because there were a lot of lone boys around in the old days. These would be brothers who might live together on rural farms. They would never have got married but would have been very loyal to one another all the same. The reason there were so many bachelor boys or lone boys was because of the way land was divided up back then. There was very little land to go around so some of the sons never left home at all. Or sometimes maybe they had no land of their own or they were living in an isolated spot and found it hard to meet someone. Back then, before everybody had cars, the houses in rural Ireland would have been miles apart. People might only see each other once a week when they went to Mass of a Sunday morning. If one of the lone boys had his eye on some girl that might be his only chance to have a chat with her. And you can't just go up to a girl and say, 'Will you marry me, love?' You can't do that. You have to go out with each other for a while and get to know one another. You have to put in a bit of an effort!

That was why the lone boys and other country people used to love to see the Travellers coming. We were their news carriers. We would have passed through other villages, meeting the locals and doing jobs for them and we knew all the latest news. They would love to see us coming and they would make a place for us by the fire so that we could tell them the latest gossip. Travellers were great storytellers as well and before the television we could spend the whole night telling stories and swapping yarns with the country people. It was a way to pass the time, especially in the winter when the nights were dark and wet.

And sometimes you'd get one of the lone boys asking you about some girl who lived on an isolated farm somewhere back along the way. And he'd be asking you what kind of a girl she was, whether she was good-hearted and funny and all the rest of it. And it was the same for single women on these farms. Sometimes the Travelling women would be nearly like their personal advisors on who would make a good husband, who was a nice man and who was hardworking.

The country people had to rely on the Travellers then because we were the only people who were travelling through the country and meeting a wide range of people. We were meeting everybody at some stage or another and so we had a better idea than most of what was going on. We were like the teletext that you have now on the television. We knew who was selling their farm, who had got a grant, who had bought new cattle. Times were different then. There was a welcome for the Traveller in those days.

The cunics and the Whidding-cén (The priests and the Church)

I mentioned earlier the bachelor boys from Mayo who lived the traditional life and who sat down to pray together in the evenings. They reminded me of my own mother. My mother, God bless her, was a very religious woman. You could say that she was 'mad for Mass'. She was always checking on us to see that we had been to Mass, to make sure that we had been to Confession and Holy Communion. When you look at Ireland nowadays you would think that religion is nearly gone. You'd notice a lot of the young people don't go to Mass anymore. It's gone from one extreme to the other.

In times gone by the priests were too strict in Ireland. They had too much power. But nowadays it's gone the opposite. It's like as if society is falling apart. There is no respect for anyone or anything. There is no respect for human life itself. Isn't there a murder nearly every day? It is hard to know what has happened to Ireland. Maybe it is because people have too much money? And then there were those scandals in the Church. They would have affected some people and caused them to lose some of their religion. Nowadays I think it is nearly up to yourself if you want to go on believing. I don't think you should change or stop believing in God because a few priests committed guilt. Let your life continue. There are a few bad apples everywhere. You can't let a bad apple affect a whole box of apples. If you had a box of apples you wouldn't deliberately put a bad apple into it would you? You can't think that way. You have to think about how to make things better and move on. When we die and we go to Heaven, please God, then everything is going to be fine anyway. Heaven is a perfect place. No bad apple is ever going to get in there and we have a promise about that.

Geiltilt of táspen (Frightened of dying)

It is a strange thing the way people nowadays never think of death. They never mention it. It's as if they are going to live forever. Isn't it strange too? Because isn't death one of the only things we are sure of in this world? 'Death and taxes', as they say. I think Travellers think of death more than people amongst the settled community. Travellers die at a younger age than the settled community do and I suppose it is not so surprising then that they think of death more often.

And a strange thing about religion. No matter how tough you are, and you say you don't believe in God and you don't believe in this, but at that last minute in your dying bed you're going to turn then whether you like it or not. Your last second, your last minute in that bed, you're going to say 'God, will you please forgive me, will you?' You can be tough all your life. You can act the tough man in this world but eventually when it comes right down to it, no matter what age you are, that's when your real fear of Satan is going to come into your body and you're going to say 'Please, will you forgive me?'

A lot of Travelling people have a deep faith. There's a deepness there. Especially losing a person. If a person dies belonging to us there's a deepness of sorrow and sadness there. You go back through the years, you'll always notice that Travelling people are always at the back of the church. They never go right down and mix in with the crowd in the seats and the benches. I don't know was it a kind of an embarrassment or shame, or the way they dressed. Everybody knows there is a difference — Travelling people and settled people. You can almost tell who's who, who is a Traveller and who is a settled person. A settled person might say, 'Well, why can't the Travelling person look like us?' That can't happen overnight. If a person is born as a Traveller that life and that roughness and that hardship is still there in their system. You can see in their faces the hardship and roughness that they've gone through. Maybe in a hundred years time it will be different. Maybe the accent and culture will be completely different. But at this present moment that Travelling culture is still there. And the sad part of it is how all the governments that were ever in this country left big families sleeping in camps on the side of the road in the muck and the squalor and the dampness and the rain and without education. And how the priests and the clergy never protested. How they never came around to campsites and said 'Lads, we'll say prayers' or something like that. How there was all this hidden religion and hidden governments that never came out to help. If you went into a convent back then you might have got a bit of grub alright. They weren't too bad. But it was very seldom that they would have gone out to a campsite. They were going across the water to Africa to try and educate over there while in their own backyard they had Travelling people and kids suffering with no education and just thrown in at the side of the road.

Poverty

There was a lot of poverty with farmers also — that's true. But it was different. There was more decency. They helped out with a bit of grub here and there — a few potatoes or whatever. They knew how we began on the road in the first place but city people didn't know this. They thought that Travellers just existed, that we were Romany Gypsies who came from a foreign country which is strange.

The tásped feen in the molly (The ghost in the camp)

I am in my fifties now. I'm old enough for a Traveller — you don't see too many elderly Travellers around now do you? — they had such hardship in their lives. Although I'm not an old man, I think, I still love to think back on the old days when Travellers had the freedom of the birds and when we were allowed to travel wherever we wished. One of my earliest memories is of when I got a fright!

I was about three or four years of age and we were camping

somewhere out near Newport in County Tipperary. Everybody was settled down in the tents for the night when this ghost came in and grabbed me by the legs! I was dragged by the ankles out of the tent and out along the ditch. Then the ghost took off the sheet that was covering his face and who was it but my father playing tricks! He had nearly frightened me half to death! All the other lads came out of the other *lúbáns* (tents) and we all had a good old *raglian* (laugh). I didn't sleep easy for a few weeks afterwards I can tell you!

The munia nuides (The good people)

In times gone by people had a great belief in those *bini nuides* (little people) they called the fairies. If people had bad luck or good luck they would explain it by what kind of relationship they had with the fairies. People would be very afraid of disturbing them in any way. If there was a fairy fort or fairy hill on someone's land they wouldn't dream of cutting the bushes on it or disturbing it. If we were looking to set up a *molly* (camp) for the night we would never dream of setting one up anywhere near where the fairies were supposed to be living. Beliefs about the fairies are still alive amongst both Travellers and settled people, although people wouldn't always admit it. Only recently a new road between Limerick and Clare had to be diverted around a fairy tree. That fairy tree had been there for generations and the construction men were frightened to tamper with it in any way.

Belief in the fairies is still there but it isn't as strong anymore. People loved telling stories about the fairies in the olden times when they told stories around the fire. When people had no radios or televisions they had a great relationship with nature and the supernatural world. They thought more deeply about the world around them than people do today. When you sit down in front of the box or the telly today, what sort of thinking do you have to do? You're like a sponge sucking in everything that you see, and a lot of what you suck in is negative. I call it the *meedil's meirigín* (the divil's box) It doesn't do you much good! The fairies were better than the box any day!

The sroidean and the dorchóg — the different glims (Morning and night — the different types of light)

As a painter I am very interested in light. There are so many different lights and so many different colours that change with the light. There is the dawn light that I see sometimes when I am painting early in the *sroidean* (morning). That light is a light that's not sure whether it wants to wake up or not. Then there is the bright afternoon light that can be harsh and hurt the *oglers* (eyes). Evening light is full of doubt and shadows. The day is going away slowly and we are moving into the secret world of the *dorchóg* (darkness). Then there is the night light of the moon, a light that is full of mystery and silence.

If you go to different parts of Ireland you can find different types of light. The light of the setting sun in the west of Ireland can be very different from the setting sun in the east or the south. As a painter I try and bring these different types of light into my work.

I think the quality of light affects our imagination. When you think of the Travellers and the settled people telling stories around the fire in the old days — how much light did they have? They were generally sitting in darkness except for the light of the fire. When they thought of that world that was beyond the fire their imaginations got to work overtime.

Nowadays we don't really know what darkness is — I am talking about real darkness. Nowadays we are blinded with light — we have too much light. The television is like a big light. If you walk through the streets at night all you can see through people's *gruinneógs* (windows) are the piercing lights of the televisions. Light and noise. When you have too much light and noise you can't really get in contact with the supernatural or the creative side of nature. Those people who sat around the fires in the past didn't have televisions and all sorts of other gadgets but they were more educated in other ways, that's for sure.

Crushing through the muinceara (Travelling through the countryside)

I was about nine years of age when I went away travelling by myself for the first time. I remember it well. I ran away from our camp in Newport on the border between Counties Limerick and Kerry and I made my way deep into the Kerry mountains. I walked most of the way and slept in farmers' hay sheds along the way. When I tell people nowadays that I ran away at such a young age, they ask me 'Were you not frightened going off by yourself like that?' 'Not a bit of it,' I say. Sure, hadn't I the richest of Traveller blood flowing through my bones. If anyone should have been able to survive on the open *tóhbar* (road) it should have been me.

I literally 'sang for my supper' along the way. I would sing the ballads my mother taught me for a lot of the country people and they gave me a meal of brown bread and buttermilk. Or I whistled tunes and played the mouth organ. People danced to my tunes on the stone hearth in a few places that I visited. Some people preferred tunes. Others preferred the ballads like *Newport Town, Carrickfergus, The Galway Shawl, Cliffs of*

Doonen. These were songs that I had learnt at the Traveller campfires from the very first moment I could hear. Then the country people would make a bed for the night for me by the open fire or in their hay-barn that would be adjacent to the farm house.

Nowadays if you were a young fella tramping the country people wouldn't let you past the front door never mind into the shed. They would be on the phone straight away to the guards or to the social services. When you went into a house back then the first thing the people would ask you was, 'Have you any story for us?' They would be mad to hear a folktale that they hadn't heard before or a joke or a bit of scandal about a councillor or a politician. And they were devils for looking for gossip about the neighbours too. They would be curious trying to find out as much as they could about their neighbours.

Since a Traveller like myself was only passing through I was the perfect person to ask about the neighbours. I might tell them the odd tidbit of information and since I would be gone again within a day or two, no-one could link me to any of the gossip! They would be saying to you, 'Were you back in such-and-such a house and did you hear anything about such-and-such a thing? Did you clean their chimney? Are that crowd back the road after buying new cattle? Is it true that so-and-so is moving home from America? Is their daughter getting dressed up to go out in the evenings at all? Is it true she's courting that old lad over in the neighbouring townland who's rotten with land and money?' As soon as you got in the door, the questions started. It was like the royal inquisition.

The geitilt (frightened) farmer and his treachery!

I remember moving along the road one evening and I hit a hill that
seemed to be going on forever. It was a bad stormy night and I knew
that I had better be making tracks about finding a farmhouse and a
bed for the night somewhere. When I got to the top of the hill the
heavens opened. The rain started to lash down and strips of lightning
flashed across the sky. I was tempted to take cover in the trees because
I didn't like the look of the lightning but I knew the rain was down for
the night. Just then I thought I could get the faint whiff of turf-smoke
from somewhere and I knew that deliverance might be at hand. 'There
must be a house around here somewhere,' I said to myself. So I started
to sprint full pelt down the hill. The night was wild and the rain was
bouncing off my coat as I turned the corner and suddenly landed in a
big farmyard.

Who was climbing over a stile from the fields but the farmer himself?
He had a hayfork and was after giving some feed to his cattle who were
all huddled together in the corner of the field, shivering with fright from
the lightning. And the farmer got a right fright to see this vision appear
from nowhere and the night as ugly and stormy as it was. He got such a
fright that he had to lean on the wall for a minute to catch his breath.
And I don't blame him because I looked a rare sight! My hair was matted
to my head with the rain and I was panting like a racehorse after running
down that hill like the devil himself.

'Where the hell did you come out of?' he said. 'Are you one of the lads
that's visiting in the cottage back the road?' 'No,' says I. 'I'm a rambler,
I'm by myself,' I says. 'Ah, for the love of God, young fella,' he says,
'where's your parents?' I said, 'They are back on the Newport side in

Tipperary.' 'And how did you get here to me?' he says. 'Did you cycle a bike or anything?' 'No,' says I. 'I'm walking, I'm rambling,' says I. 'I'm just looking to make a few shillings as I go along.' 'Man, but you gave me a fright there,' he says. And I said to him then, 'Will you tell me this, is there any old place that I could put my head down for the night? Have you any old hay barns? The old shed will do me there.' I pointed to a corrugated roof shed that was the far side of the farmyard.

'Well, the one place that I can't leave you into is the last shed,' says the farmer, 'because there is a bull in there and I leave him around the old yard to keep an eye on the old house. I let him out when I go up the road to meet Katie. He wouldn't take too kindly to sharing his quarters.' 'Who is Katie?' I piped up, thinking she was probably the girl he was courting or something! He didn't give me an answer though. 'I'll tell you what I'll do,' he said. 'I have an old Volkswagen car. Hop into the car there and I'll bring you down to my neighbour's house.' So he let me into the car and we drove down the road, a good half a mile or so away from where his own house was. He parked his car well back from the house and he said to me, 'See that hay barn there,' he says, 'that's Murphy's hay barn. Just go in there and whatever you do—if you get caught or anything in the morning don't tell him that I sent you in!'

Then he produced two cuts of *durra* (bread) and *gelum* (butter) from the pocket of his coat and handed them to me before I left the car. I remember that as if it happened yesterday as I was absolutely starving with the hunger. He drove quietly away and I walked slowly down the road gobbling down the food like a Robinson Crusoe who's just found a real loaf of bread. And jay! but the food was grand. I didn't even notice the storm still pelting around me I was so engrossed in the beautiful cuts of soda bread. There was a little hinge-lock on the door of the shed but my small child's fingers were able to prise it open, no problem. I stumbled around in the dark for a few minutes but I soon found the side of the barn where the hay was stored. I made a little manger for myself in the hay and I was asleep in no time. The rhythm that the drumming rain was making on the corrugated roof had me asleep in no time.

Many is the night that I spent in a hay barn and I can honestly say that there was rarely a time that I wasn't asleep in a matter of minutes. There's nothing like walking miles, eating brown bread and the smell of hay to help you nod off! My plan was to get out of the shed before the farmer did his rounds the next morning but I got so comfy that I fell into a deep sleep and didn't wake up in time. Sure enough didn't his dog sense me in there the next morning. He started barking and your man came out and found me there. 'Where in the heck did you come out of?' he said. 'Your neighbour above the road there sent me down,' I told him. 'Did he now?' says he. 'There's going to be trouble here,' I said to myself, 'I better skedaddle.' I said I was going and your man let me off. But I often wondered about those two farmers afterwards. Did they have a good old row about the one fella betraying the other and driving me down there to boot!

If you go back through the old stories `in Ireland, it was the traitor who was the most hated man, especially in those centuries that we were persecuted and colonised by the British. There was always the odd bit of traitorism knocking around! That farmer was a prime example!

My dhíls mistling along the muinceara tóhbars (Travelling alone along the country roads)

I spent a good while during my youth rambling by myself. I preferred it that way. I could appreciate nature better by myself and it was travelling through the landscapes of my youth that I got a lot of the inspiration for my paintings. I love to paint rural scenes, the cottage, the fire, the half-door, the sea, trees and water in all their wildness. I remember reading about the old poets in Ireland long ago. They used to go to a lonely hut on the side of a mountain or out into a lonely glen to do their thinking and compose their poetry. They needed the complete silence and the solitary feeling of nature to compose at their best. When they were finished composing the poem in their heads, they would head back to where they were staying so as to write out or sing their poem.

Swurcin' the sorcáns (singing songs) for a living

Rambling through the countryside was a great way for me to learn and to grow. I learnt how to survive and to make a living and I was only nine years of age. I could make my few shillings from the music and the singing and in this way I was my own boss. I was reliant on no-one but myself. On a day where I couldn't make any money from the music I could always *géig* (beg) a piece of *durra* (bread) or a cup of *weed* (tea) at some farmer's house. One advantage of travelling solo was that it was a lot easier to make money ballad-singing and musicking when you were on your own than if you were with a couple of people. When a couple of musicians or singers are together whatever money *grade* (money) you make has to be divided by two or three and it is not so easy to survive then.

The one drawback of travelling alone is that you have too much time to think. It could be very lonely at night sometimes. You could be lying there alone in some hay barn and you would start thinking about your family and your life. I would start wondering where my family were camped or whether they were alright. At that time I knew that if I got really lonely I would always find them somewhere up around the Newport or Cappamore areas. They wouldn't go travelling up to the west of Ireland while I was on the road—they would wait for me to come back. When I first starting my rambling away from camp my parents were a bit worried about me. But they got so used to me that they would say, 'That fella, that's just the way he is. Sure, what could happen to him? He's not going to get murdered and he won't get kidnapped either because there's nothin' there!' So after a while they really weren't too worried. They knew that I was a good musician and that I would never starve then.

I always had at least one mouth organ hidden in the folds of my coat so as to preserve it from the damp and I would sing and play. I always had a fair repertoire of tunes that I could play. I had learnt them all from my mother's side of the family. They had come with the mother's milk as they say! I'd play *The Whistling Gypsy, The Lonesome Boatman,* or other tunes of a similar style. I would put a lot of emotion and feeling into the ballads and the tunes. I remember seeing country people wipe away tears from their eyes when I was singing, they were that affected. I had learnt the singing trade calling to the *céns* (houses) with my mother. She had a great voice altogether. Her voice was in the style of the great Bridie Gallagher who used to sing *The Homes of Donegal.* She had a similar style also to Delia Murphy or the great Traveller singer Margaret

Barry, ballad-singers who could belt out a tune and stop people in their tracks!

The old couple in Kerry

I knew this couple one time and they lived up in the mountains of Kerry. I was a lonely drifter at the time, just my bag on my back. I was looking for work and I just came to this dreary old cottage. I knocked on the half-door and inside were the grandest old couple that you could see. They were in their eighties at least. She was sitting at the open fire, with a shawl around her shoulder, and he sitting opposite with a bottle of water in his hand. At least that's what I thought it was, but in fact it was poitín. And in a polite and gentlemanly manner they asked me to enter. 'Come close to the fire and warm yourself.' 'God bless you,' I said, 'and your kindness.' 'Did you come far?' he asked. 'Oh, from Killarney,' I replied. 'Killarney, by God?' 'Yes,' I replied. 'You must be worn out. Here, will you have a drop of that? It will warm you up, so it will.' Well, I drank strong drink in my time, but this drink beat them all. It was that strong that the tears came from my eyes.

'We don't get many visitors here, you know.' He spoke in a happy voice. 'In fact you're the only one in months except for the postman. And even he's too lazy to come up the hill.' 'I suppose if you gave him a sup of that old stuff, I'm sure he would move,' I said. As the night arrived slowly our heads began to spin. Instead of looking at two people I was looking at four. I played on my mouth organ the whole night through.

And we had a grand old time. If the world could be like these two old souls what a world it would be! They put me up in the hayshed that night and it felt warm and grand throughout the night. I could hear the farmers shooting the foxes from the hills but I was comfortable that night. The rain was beating off the tin roof giving me that relaxing feeling. The next morning the cock woke me up. I did not want to rise. I was too warm. The old folks were asleep or so I thought. In fact they were gone to Mass. They left a note for me beside me, stating, 'Call again sometime. Going to the Church and God bless you on your journey.' And right beside the note was a breakfast. How kind they were. I could never forget them. I often wondered how they had got to the church — probably a donkey and cart. They were surely tough. Some day I would love to go back but they are probably well dead and gone and I'm sure that there is a bed in Heaven for them.

It was tough going — travelling over the mountains of Kerry. But what a beautiful place Kerry is. I call it a little bit of Heaven. There are places there that are untouched by man. I got a bit of work from one farm to another. From time to time I had nothing to eat of course. A raw head of cabbage or a carrot from a garden was all I ate but still I was alive. Being a rover gave me the opportunity to see the beauty of Ireland. Walking up the laneways and side-roads. There are so many things to see. I often stopped to watch an old man building a stone wall along his field and how he took pride in his work. Great patience and determination.

Well, I did my bit of roving around Kerry and it was a pleasure to have seen what I had seen. Giving me that peace of mind. Such beauty does not slip from one's mind too quickly.

Going to the big smoke

It was soon after leaving Kerry that I hitched a lift to Dublin. This city was big. Boy, was it big! The question I asked myself was: Is it too big for me? Would I get the hang of it? I had relations in Dublin but to find them was another matter. I preferred to do my own thing anyway, to work alone and make whatever few shillings I could. I was by myself at the time but I would often stay on a campsite with other Travellers then. I decided to buy some tools and work as a sharpener. So I bought files and ringes and I went out sharpening for myself. I was sharpening all sorts of things — clippers, lawnmowers, knives — and there was plenty of work. The trick was to sharpen someone's lawnmower out in the footpath so that the next-door neighbour saw you. They might come out and say, 'Give us an ould shout there when you're finished. You might do mine as well.' At first it took sometime to learn this trade but I learned; as Frank Sinatra said, — 'I did it my way' and so I did.

There is plenty of work in this country and we don't need the government to help us once you are willing and able. I pity all these young people who try hard to learn and got to the top schools, giving it their best and the sad thing is — is there anything for them when they have passed their exams? All that education and knowledge. Those young people who put their hearts and souls into their work. Surely they deserve the best.

A tradesman's surdu (A tradesman's work)

While there was huge hardship involved in the Travelling life I would be telling a lie if I didn't say that it was also in another sense a very romantic life. We were a free people for part of the year at least and free to roam the country in our horse-drawn caravans. I remember sitting beside my father at the front of the wagon as he steered the horses along the boreens. We were at a height and we could see out over the countryside on either side. We owned no land and yet we were masters of all we surveyed. We could appreciate the beauty of the land as the *currys* (horses) clip-clopped slowly along and this formed the artist in me, I suppose. I had a sense of the beauty that lay in the land, the rolling meadows, the old thatched houses and the sight of the ordinary country man working upon the land.

Those summers where my family travelled between farms in search of work were what moulded me as an artist. My mother was a singer and so she was an artist in her own right. But I think the painting gene came from both sides of my family. My father was a very skilled tinsmith. He was great with his hands, a craftsman in every sense of the word. My mother liked to write and to draw. She was a sketcher, always sketching little pictures of birds and other animals. So you could say with regard to my painting talent that 'it wasn't from the wind that I got it'. As a child you imitate your parents and I probably copied both of them to a degree in my early development as an artist. I was always curious so I would be sitting there asking my mother questions. 'What kind of a bird is that that you are drawing? What's that that you are writing? What's that that you are reading in the paper?'

Watching a real tinsmith in action was like watching a painter or sculptor at work—it was real craftsmanship that was handed down between the generations. With my father I would always be watching him at work with the tin and the solder. I would watch the speed of his hands as he worked with the tin, the strength of his fingers as he twisted and bent the tin into shape. I would work the bellows sometimes while he would work the ladle and whatever fuel we had.

He would fit a piece of tin that he measured up to the hole where it needed to be added. Then he had what was called a 'dam' where you would put the molten metal so as to confine it where you wanted it. The molten metal would be poured over the broken area then and when it cooled he would shape it. Sometimes he used a soldering iron to smooth the metal into shape. People used to say 'I couldn't give a tinker's dam' about something or other thinking that this was a curse of some kind. But what they didn't realise was that a tinker's dam was a very important part of a tinsmith's equipment. Sometimes it might only be a small hole scooped into the dust or sand on the roadside where the tinsmith was working. Every now and then the tinsmith would dip a piece of solder into this dam while rubbing his hot soldering iron in the sand so as to clean it. He could then use his iron to pick up the solder from the dam and then spread it over the bit of tin or copper he was working on.

When he had finished a job, I remember my father carefully tapping with his hammer to make sure the gallon can or tin bucket was as right as rain. When he made his own buckets I used to walk behind him from farm to farm. He would have a collection of newly-shining buckets hanging on a rope from his shoulder. We made a right racket between us. People would hear us coming and come out to the half-doors.

Painting in the liba (blood)

Artistry was all around me and yet in spite of this I didn't actually become an artist myself until later in life. If someone had given me some paints and brushes as a young lad I think I would probably have started painting for real years ago. But it wasn't until I was in my thirties that I painted my first real painting. Since then I haven't stopped working. Morning, noon and night! It's like the brush and myself are trying to make up for all those years when we didn't know one another. We're like one of those married couples that you don't see one without the other. In the past twenty years I have produced at least six hundred oil paintings, paintings that have been sold all over Ireland. A few of my paintings have also gone across the water to England or America, usually with Irish people who want to carry an image of the Irish landscape with them back to their country of exile. A little image of home in a faraway place.

I discovered my talent by pure accident! I was sitting in the house talking to a friend of mine and I was scribbling and sketching as I spoke to him, as I often did. I often would be sketching away with an old pencil as I would be having the chat with someone, just out of habit. Anyway this friend of mine arrived down to me the very next morning and he plonked a set of paints and brushes on the table in front of me. Then he went out to his car and what did he bring in but a canvas. 'What's this?' I said. 'What do you think it is?' he said. 'It's time for you to move on from the pencils and the sketching. There's a panel and a canvas. Now, I'm going to go away again and you are going to do your first painting.' I was a bit stunned and so I piped up, 'What'll I draw?' 'You won't draw anything,' says he. 'You are going to paint now and you are going to paint whatever comes to mind. Next time I come back I'll know I'll be seeing a nice painting in front of me.' And with that he was gone out the door.

The *rodas* (door) was still shaking after him when I took the brushes in my hands and I haven't stopped painting since. I decided to start with nature scenes that first day and to be honest they are my favourite to this day. I remember mixing the paint and looking out the *gruinneóg* (window) at the streets of the *helm* (town) on that first day of my apprenticeship. My *oglers* (eyes) saw the streets outside but my mind's eye saw something else completely.

SOME OF MY PAINTINGS

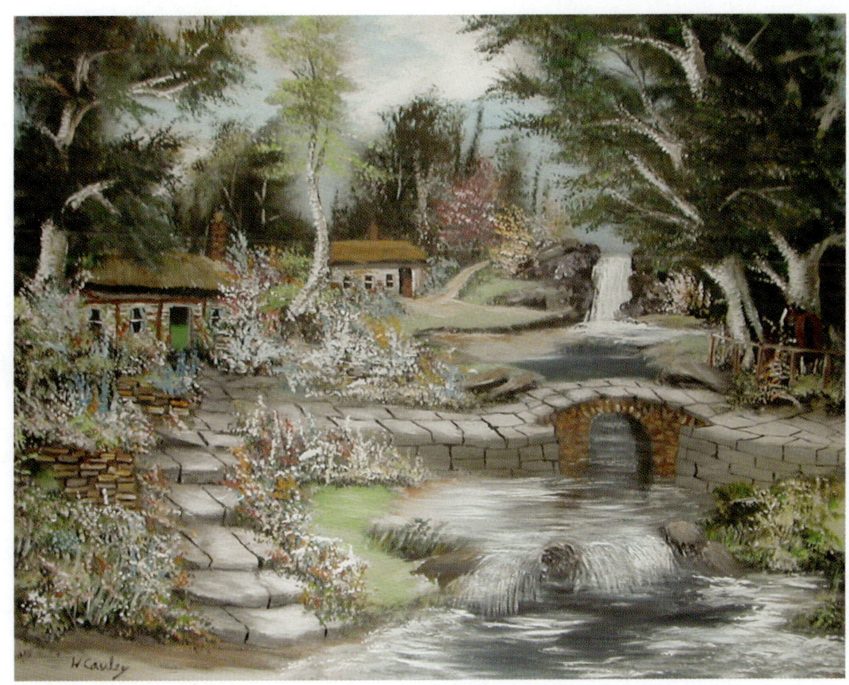

1. 'Blossom Hollow'. This is a scene from my imagination.
(August 2004)

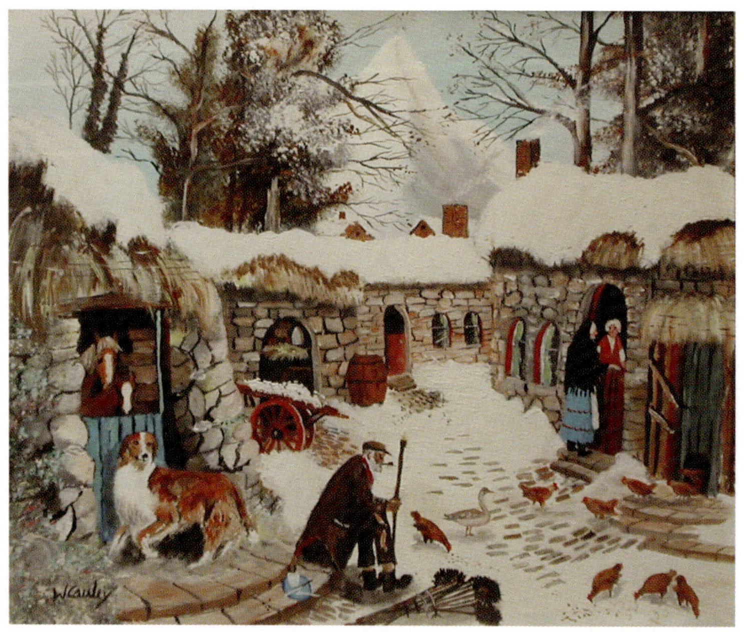

2. 'A Country Rover'. I painted this two years ago, at Christmas, in memory of my father. The woman wearing the shawl is the rover's wife; she is *geigin'* (begging) at the door.

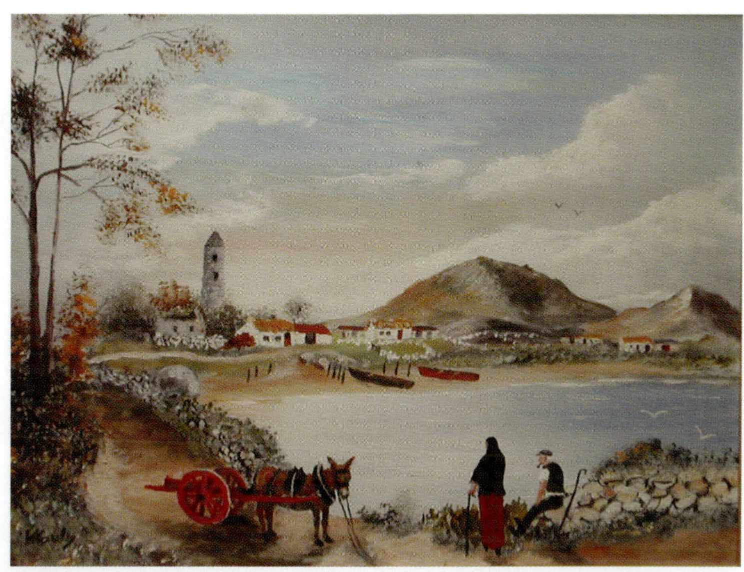

3. 'Old Country Flames'. The two old people are old flames—they used to go out with one another when they were young. They are now looking down at the village where they grew up and having a chat and recalling some memories of their youth.

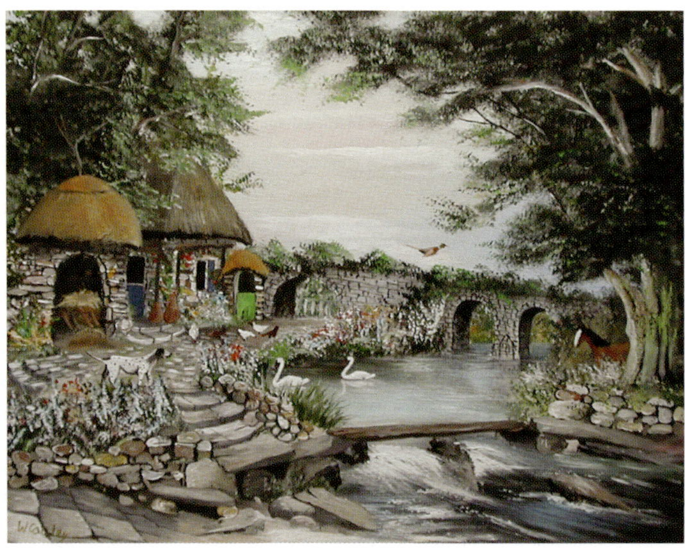

4. 'Flagstone Cottage'. The flags and cobbles are a
reminder of the past, of the way the streets used to be.
(July 2004)

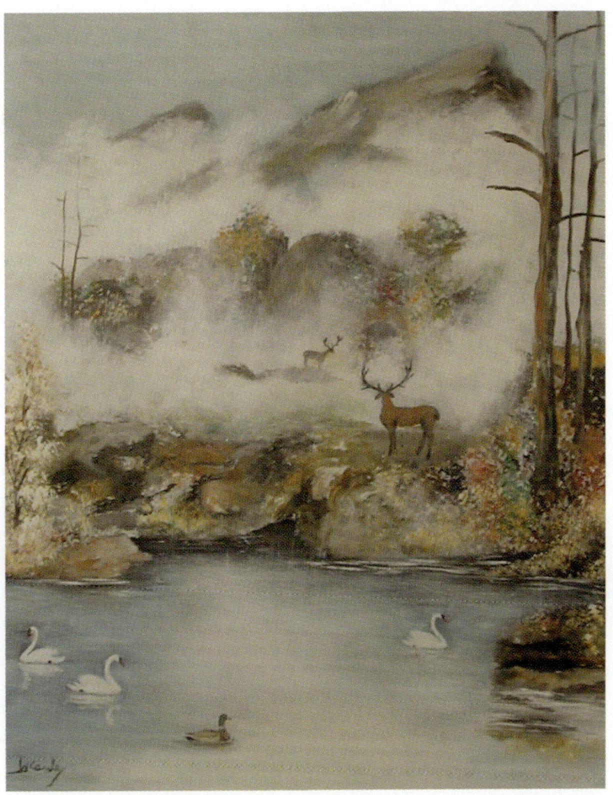

5. 'Misty mountain'. For me this shows the
freedom of nature — there are no human beings
in this scene, intruding on and destroying nature.

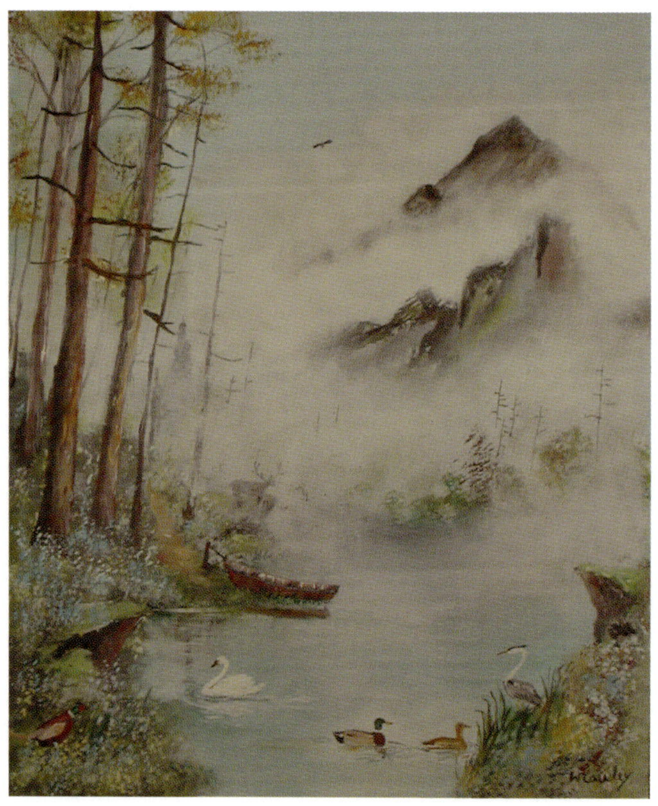

6. 'Born Free'. I painted this from my imagination. The heron—a beautiful and peaceful bird—is fishing quietly by the lake.

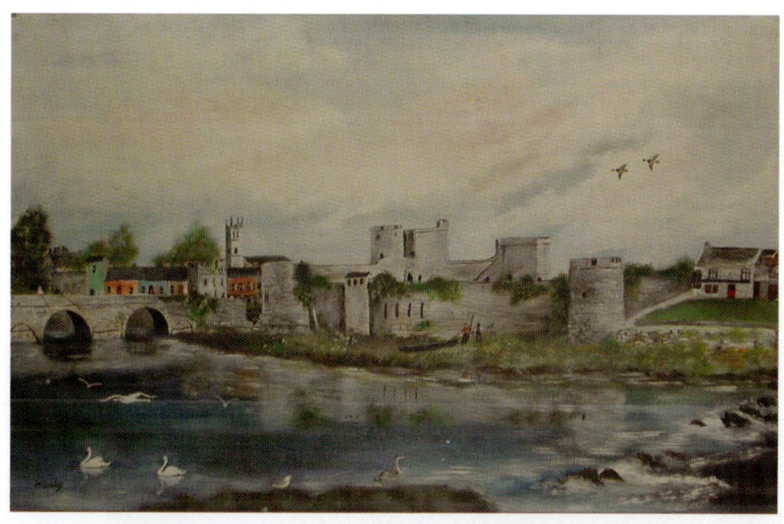

7. 'King John's Castle'. The inspiration for this was the city of
Limerick. Limerick is a big part of my life.

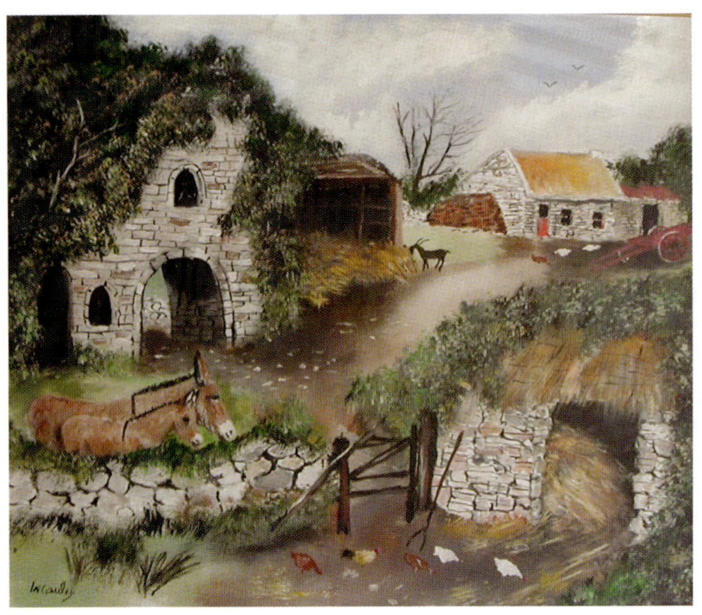

8. 'An Irish cottage'. An image of rural Ireland — a rural
Ireland that has nearly faded away.

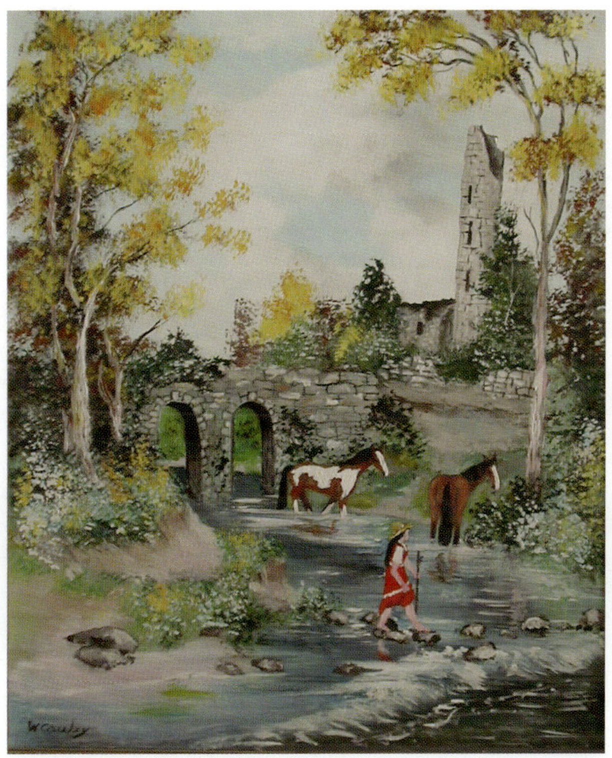

9. 'Rambling Lily'. I have a daughter called Lily. In this picture she's walking across the river, she's free, she's walking wherever she pleases — like a Travelling girl. It represents the freedom that Travelling people should have if the world was fairer.

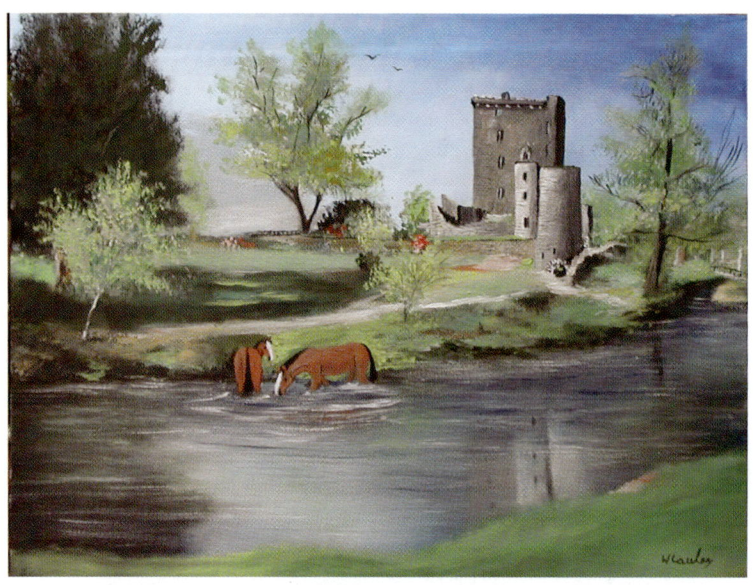

10. 'Old Blarney'. The castle in this picture is based on an image in my mind of Blarney Castle, a fine castle in the Munster region.

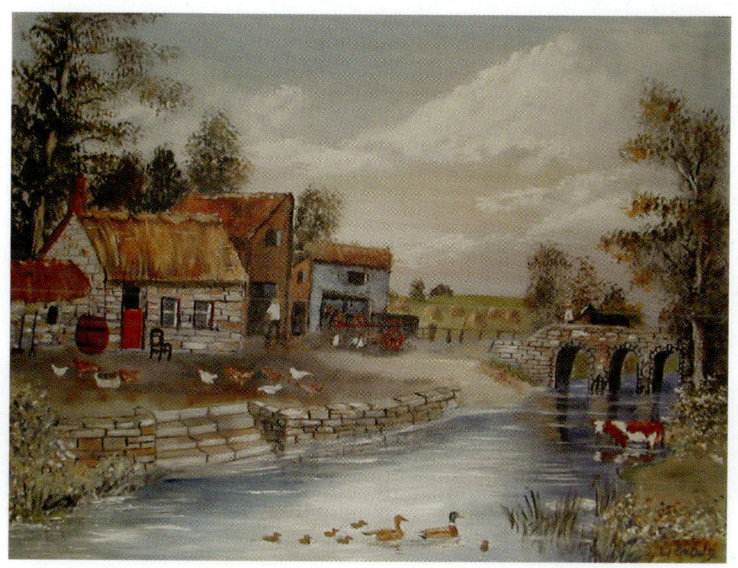

11. 'An Irish farm'. This painting is based on what I saw when I was rambling as a youth: it's a scene that I saw at that time and it stuck in my mind. (1998–9)

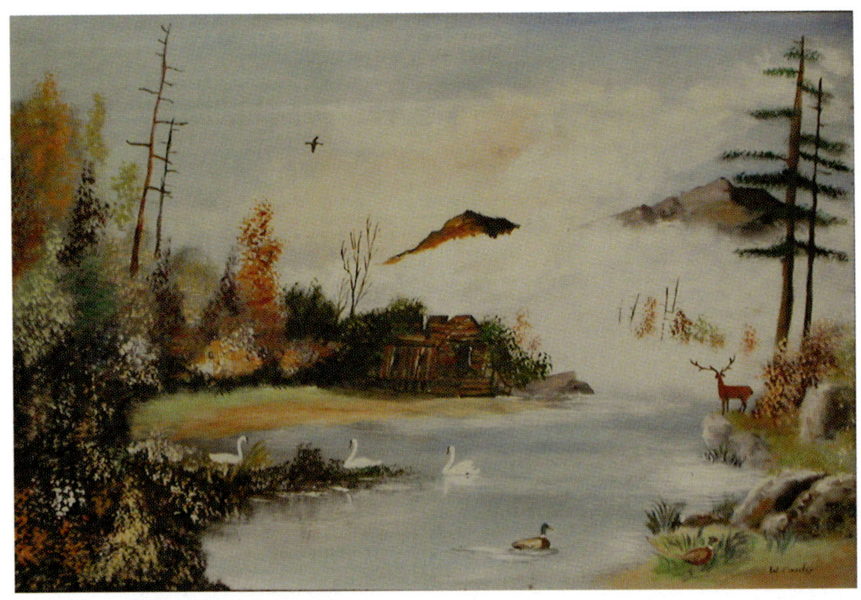

12. 'A Land Far Away'. It is an image of nature undisturbed and as it should be—nature as a wilderness.

The image that came to mind for my first painting was of a huge wild ocean and the currachs bobbing on the waves. I thought of the Aran Island people and the Connemara people and the wildness of their existence by the sea. And I began to paint the fishermen and their combat with the sea.

And that was the subject of my very first painting. It's a theme that I have returned to in my paintings over the years. I remember seeing the Connemara people and the other island people of Galway and Mayo when my family were travelling that part of the country and I only a *gália* (child). And they must have made a big impression on me, those west of Ireland people, because I can still bring them to mind like it was only yesterday. Those western people were the toughest people. They were a hard people, a rare people. In a funny kind of way they were something like the Travelling people who are a rare people also. When my family travelled back around Connemara in the fifties and sixties, the land was rocky and poor. The people were poor too but they were a unique people also. Like Travellers they were able to survive against all the odds. Back then I often saw men out in the wildest of seas and the waves so big they looked like their currach would be swallowed up in a moment.

I remember one day that I ran away from the camp early in the morning. I wanted to avoid doing some of the jobs around the *molly* (camp) that you had to do in the mornings. So I shinned my way up these rocks that overlooked the sea until I came to the edge of a cliff. And I remember crawling towards the edge on my stomach and looking down. And what did I see but these two lads in a currach and they were rowing out towards the sea. They were like two dots from where I was sitting and for every few foot of progress they made they seemed to be thrown back again by these huge waves. I remember sitting there watching them for an age and their progress out to sea seemed so slow. Or at least that was the way it looked from where I was sitting. But they were fighters. They kept at it and eventually they got away from the rocks that were at the bottom of the cliff. After a while they disappeared from view altogether. Those islandmen were true and willing fishermen. Any man that puts his life at risk just to feed his family deserves the greatest respect. Little did those two Connemara men know as I spied on them then that they would be the image to appear on my very first canvas all of twenty-five years later.

A gift from Dalyon (God)

I was happy with my first painting of the Connemara men battling with the elements. Everybody said to me, 'It's great, Willy, fair play to you!' and all the rest of it. But I knew deep down that it was no masterpiece. Like every painter it would take me a while to get used to the textures and moods of the oils, the sway of the brush and different shades of light and dark. With each painting I did, I began to improve. It took time and effort but eventually my painting technique started to get better and the paintings began to come together more naturally. It was just a matter of time before the hundreds of images and scenes that I had stored in my childhood memory progressed out through me. They had to, I suppose, because they were meant to come alive somewhere.

Those paintings were meant to be in the same way that I was meant to be an artist. It was meant to be. That's my feeling about it and that is the only way that I can explain how I came to discover my artistic vocation later on in life. There was no such thing as me practicing for years to become an artist. There was no such thing as a person teaching me and training me in techniques for years on end. These things didn't happen because they weren't meant to happen. The painting was meant to be. That gift was meant to appear when it did. It is very simple in a way — either the gift appears or it doesn't. It is like the timber worker who can create something beautiful out of a piece of wood. Or a songwriter or a poet. All these artists can create something because they have been given a gift. The way I see things is that God has given me a gift. In fact He has given me a loan of that gift really. The gift is on loan for a while and when He wants to take that gift back again, He will. You see a lot of pride and snobbery in the art world. But the thing about being an artist is that self-pride is no pride. The gift was never yours in the first place. It belongs to the Man Above and he'll take it away again when the time comes. Maybe he'll pass the gift onto someone else in the family? Who knows? He might pass it on to someone in my own family.

My mother lived just long enough to see that I had become a painter. She saw only two of my paintings. But she told me before she died that she was delighted that I had discovered this talent and become a painter. She wasn't so surprised that the talent had appeared when it did. I think that she had an inkling that the talent was there, that it was in the blood going back through the generations. She was probably wondering when it was going to happen, when it was going to come through.

Finding my munia tóhbar (chosen path) through life

A FORGOTTEN CHILD

Slowly but slowly
The morn comes to light
As raindrops fall and fall
Upon my canvas roof
My tent is small and bed of straw
A blanket damp and mouldy
And I but a lad, a hungry lad
So weak and small
Born to life, free and wild
My eyes swollen and red
From smoke of the camp fire
On that late, late night . . .
But to rise, and to rise
To the early morning light
Brings all but joy
For the shivering night has passed
And the heating sun has risen
To glow upon my frozen frame
And bring me to life once more
I, a lad, a roving lad
A forgotten and wandering child.

Discovering painting made my life complete in a way. I described
the camping life and my wanderings alone earlier in this story. I liked
both the solitude of wandering the countryside alone and the opposite
of that too — the company that the travelling and camping life brought
with it. But there were hard times too, times when I cried out with the
suffering that poverty brought. When I was only a very young boy of

five or six years of age I can remember that I often cried out to God. Sometimes I was angry with Him. 'Why did you let me be born?' I'd say. 'Take me out of this life. This life of hunger and misery. This life of sadness. Sleeping in a tent with damp straw and water flowing under my back, and the night-rats crawling close by in the darkness.' Later on I forgave God for letting me be born into a life of such hardship. There was a reason why I was on this earth after all. And that reason was to paint nature, to paint the creatures of this earth, her trees and her landscapes.

A noiceall in the dorchóg (A candle in the darkness)

I suppose it is true to say that everyone is born with a gift of one kind or another. I knew a man once and he had a wonderful gift. If you gave him a piece of timber or bog oak he carved it into a wonderful shape. He could create a masterpiece in a matter of minutes, right as you were watching him. There are so many people out there with these gifts. God did not forget anyone because everyone is special to Him. But to find that gift and to build on it is the secret that you have to discover in life. To control that gift, but most of all not to waste it. I myself never knew that I had this gift until later in my life. Sure, I had always sketched with pencils when I was a young lad and I had noticed that deep inner feeling of joy I felt when I was sketching. My first paintings did not look like much but to me they had meaning. As time went by, my inspiration to paint grew stronger and stronger and at one stage I was painting three paintings a day. And all my paintings were done by candlelight at first. People would say to me, 'Why do you do your paintings by candlelight?'

There were two answers to that. First, we had no electricity when I started painting so I had no choice. Second, the family would be asleep at night so it was the best time to work. I would have peace and quiet. It is difficult to paint or do any kind of art work if you have distractions. I used to go out to where the caravan is parked outside the house. It was quiet and peaceful there. A caravan of silence. I definitely damaged my eyesight working by candlelight. But I couldn't put a brake on this will to paint. The paintings were like pictures in my mind and they were waiting to be put on canvas. The landscapes were crying out to me: 'Please paint us before it is too late.'

Falling to culdrum (Falling asleep)

I often wore myself out painting. Night after night I would be there in the shadow, hunched over the easel. There is many a time that I fell asleep while painting. The brush would be lingering off my fingers, the candles would have flickered to ends. I think that each time I paint, a piece of me is gone. The urge to paint never seems to stop and every time an image of a landscape comes into my mind I know that I have to do that painting right there and then. It doesn't matter what time of the day or night it is because if I don't paint it there and then, it just vanishes from my mind. In other words I've just wasted God's gift and His scenery. I hope that my paintings have made people happy. When many people see a particular landscape in a painting it brings memories floating back to them.

Getting a 'block' at the painting

I might get a bit panicky the odd time when I am working on a painting. It happens to everybody who is trying to create something new. I might say to myself, 'OK, I'm after putting a person over in this part of the painting. Now I'll put him over here and take her over there', and I might change the whole lot around! And it often happens to me that I might stay up the whole night completing a landscape. I will be as happy as Larry going to bed, feeling very satisfied with my work. Then I'll wake up the next morning and decide I don't really like what I've done at all. And I might have to change the whole lot again. I suppose you could say that it depends on whatever mood you are in. I might look at a painting there and get browned off with it and I might say to myself, 'It didn't turn out as good there as I thought.' And the more I would look at it the more the urge would come on me to start making changes to it. I might start to get bored with the painting and decide to put more characters in or more colour or 'I'll put a waterfall over in that part of the painting' or whatever. So there's a sense in which a painting is never finished. It might change again in the future. You're never finished with anything in this life!

Painting for the séids (gardaí)

Every artist has their own skills. Abstract painting is something that I never could get into. I've been painting landscapes for so long that I could not change now. I just love the land and all its creatures on it. I often wore my brushes to the end. And believe it or not I often cut my own hair to make a brush. It makes no difference. It works for me. Well, you didn't expect me to cut off my wife's hair, did you? Well, did you? Of course, if I had an old fox or a goat—now that would be something else, so it would!

When I was living with my wife and children on the canal bank in Limerick we were living in a caravan at the time. The Gardaí used to bring me down photos of their local homestead or postcards of the Rock of Cashel or places in County Clare. And I would paint for them. There was one time when I had a terrible hangover and to be quite honest I was stone broke—for I hadn't the price of a cure. Well, I was walking down Parnell Street in Limerick City and I was across the road from the Red Rose Café. There was a patrol car parked outside the Red Rose Café. The two gardaí were inside the café having their breakfast. I stood right across the street waiting for them to come out and after a while I spotted them leaving the café. I shouted 'Hello' over to them. They saluted me back 'How are you, Willy?' Well, I said to myself. 'So far, so good. At least these lads know me.' 'Will ye do me a favour?' I said. 'What's that?' they asked. 'Will you give me a loan of a tenner? You see, I'm currently doing a painting for one of your colleagues and you can get the tenner back off him.' Well, the garda looked baffled. He gave me the tenner as it happens and I haven't seen the same man since.

I was a kind of a rogue at times but I was never really trying to offend anyone. Like a lot of painters I would use whatever was to hand to do my painting when inspiration struck and when I was short of materials. I often painted on bread trays and all the delivery men in the city knew me. I would paint on 'Pat the Baker' trays and 'Irish Pride' trays. In fact I painted on anything that I could get my hands on.

A loner painter

I mentioned my father earlier in this book. He was a bit of a loner—he was happiest travelling out the country and away from the hustle and bustle of the city. I suppose you could say that I take after him—he was a craftsman with the tin. He was creating something new with the tin in the same way that I create something new every time I stand in front of a blank canvas. Like my father too, I am a bit of a loner in an artistic sense. I know a few artists around the city here and they are all lovely people but I don't really want to be part of any art scene. I have been invited to art galleries and exhibitions over the years but I prefer to stay at home and keep working. I want to let the painting let me drift towards what's right for me. If I went to art galleries and exhibitions and all the rest of it I think my mind would start to change and my own painting style would be affected. Some artists see other paintings and they go mad trying to change their style and then they end up torn between their own natural style and someone else's and it does them more harm than good. I prefer painting landscapes and I just want to keep drawing on my memories of rural Irish scenes that I remember from when I was a young lad. There are so many scenes in my mind just waiting to be painted if God gives me the time.

I have no real interest in all this modern art — where you splash paint here and throw paint at the canvas there — and it is suddenly worth five million quid! Maybe I should cut off my right ear like Vincent Van Gogh and the prices of my paintings might go through the roof! Poor Vincent Van Gogh knew suffering and hardship too, the poor misfortunate. He died penniless and now his paintings are worth millions. Why didn't he say to God when he was dying, 'God, will you please reincarnate me and I'll have a part of that money?' People often say that they wouldn't like to be reincarnated but if there was such a thing as reincarnation I myself would love to come back and that's the truth!

I would love to come back and be reincarnated into the travelling life the way it once was except that this time I would be making the rules about where I could travel and where I couldn't. It would be Willy

Cauley's law that would rule, not the government's. I would say 'I want to set my caravan in this place tonight and I want to camp there tomorrow night. And in a few weeks' time I want to camp down in Kerry!' And the government wouldn't be able to say to me 'You can't park there — there's a big boulder there — you can't go in there now!'

Travellers — normal Irish nuides (people)

Sometimes in this country they treat you like an alien because you are a Traveller. Some settled people react so badly towards Travellers that you almost feel you have come from some other planet but nobody told you. That's how bad-minded some people are towards Travellers. They hate us for some unexplained reason. In my time I have been mocked and jeered at, because I am a Traveller. But I got used to it and later on I passed no heed to them. Nowadays most people respect me both as an artist and because they find me a quiet, friendly person. There are other people however who never seem to get over their prejudices. Maybe someday they will understand that people like myself are their brothers in this life, that we are all God's children, brothers and sisters.

As a Traveller child I was always aware of the different way that people looked at you. When I went to Mass at the country villages I always stood at the back of the church for if I had gone closer to the altar I'd have got the feeling that I was being watched. We Travellers are a different people so we stand out from the crowd. People think because we have a different culture that there is something wrong with us. It is sad but that is the way that life is. And the strangest thing of all is that Travelling people and settled people are often buried beside one another when we pass on. Is that the only time that we communicate with each other? You have Cauleys in this country for centuries — there are Cauleys who are settled people and Cauleys who are Travelling people. Do you mean to tell me that the settled Cauleys and the Travelling Cauleys aren't related somewhere back along the line? Of course they are. But so many settled people act as if we, the Travellers never had any connection with them.

It's like President Kennedy, President Clinton or President Reagan in America. It's pretty obvious from their names that they are related to people back here in Ireland somewhere back though the generations. Even Pierce Brosnan — I doubt if he was born James Bond! There are connections between all the Irish families if you look back through the history records — whether you are a McCarthy, an O'Driscoll, an O'Reilly, a Cauley or any other name that is common amongst the Travellers here in Munster. If they are not Irish names then I will have to go back to whatever planet I'm supposed to have landed from!

Rush-hour in the Emerald Isle

Everybody's world has changed in Ireland. Whether you are a settled person or a Traveller, it is all change. Our world has became too modern, too fast. Everything's a rush. It's all this 'Close the door, watch the box (telly), press the button there. We'll get Sky, BBC, every channel under the sun.' Everybody is in a mad rush all the time. Where they are going to I don't know. The hours on the clock go by at the same speed as they did one hundred years ago or even a thousand years ago. The time that God made is still the same.

I remember the old people who hung onto their sense of time as best they could, the ones who refused to change. I remember an old man named John McCarthy. He was a loner, a Travelling man. He was a lovely person who died about ten years ago, may he rest in peace. He used to go from place to place with his donkey and a cart. He travelled all around the outskirts of Limerick, Tipperary, especially the Newport side of Tipperary. And he never rushed. He always had time for everybody whether they were a Traveller or a settled person. He treated everyone the same, as we're all supposed to do. He was a tinsmith originally and people loved to see him coming, he was such a gentleman.

I remember going into a house with him one time a good few years back. The two of us were cleaning chimneys. This woman sat us down at the table when we were finished working and she started to fill up the kettle for a *dreep* of *weed* (drop of tea). And she started opening a packet of teabags. Teabags were only a new thing back then and John McCarthy said to her as politely as he could, 'Ma'am, will you leave out the old tay-bags. Will you give me the old tea. Just a few spoons. Don't put no tay-bags in, whatever you do.' And the woman of the house put in the old tea without a bother.

John McCarthy was one of these people who had the old habits. The tea was one thing but he never got used to motor cars either. He would say to me, 'Willy,' he'd say, 'look at the motor cars there. They're unnatural. I'm afraid to cross that road, with the speed of them.' And the strange thing was — he never would cross the road either! He would simply keep going and going without crossing the road for fear his donkey might get killed. John McCarthy is gone now, God be good to him. The world he belonged to is gone now too. He stuck to the old ways and never changed. That was his life until he died. He was a rare piece of iron — a unique character from the Travelling people.

A changing muinceara (A changing country)

As an artist you are always looking at the world around you. And that world is changing at an unbelievable speed as well. There is digging and building everywhere. There are camping places that my family used to return to year after year according to our tradition and they are already unrecognisable. Everywhere there is digging and building. Everywhere there are new houses and roads. The countryside is changing and when the countryside changes the people who live in that countryside change too. Throughout my life I have adored the beauty of Ireland, its waterfalls, its mountains and its valleys. I think of my country, Mother Ireland, and how it is changing so fast. Will there come a time when all these valleys and glens will be covered with buildings? No room for a cuckoo or a bird to nest. No beauty for a child to see. Just buildings reaching to the very heavens. I will be well gone when that time comes but I pity the young ones then.

We all live in the cities now and I wonder will many children in the future only see pictures of nature hanging on the wall? And will they wonder and point at the pictures? What's that creature there? And is that supposed to be a hill or a mountain? And is that a waterfall? I grew up surrounded by nature and I walked across fields in my bare feet. I was lucky to see nature as few people today get to see it. I listened to the corncrake out on the meadow, I heard the trickle of water in the streams. Many's the time I saw a fox running over the hills that were like heather. Ireland has often treated my community badly but I am still proud of her. When I pass away I hope that it will be here in my own dear country. I would like them to lay me down on a hill that overlooks a valley. That would be a dream of mine.

In Rispún (In the Borstal)

I was sent to a Borstal in Letterfrack, County Galway for four years in 1966. I went in when I was only twelve years of age and came out again when I was sixteen. That Borstal was the cruellest and most horrible place I ever had the misfortune to spend time in.

I have no wish to describe the punishments that went on in these Borstals because they only bring back terrible memories. Some children were beaten with sticks and leather straps. Others were punished by being soaked in freezing cold baths. To even mention the name Letterfrack, brings nightmares for some of the lads who spent time there.

I recently went off camping with my sons to the west of Ireland and I went back to Letterfrack again to try and put the ghosts in my mind at rest. I took some photos of the graveyard where so many young lads are buried. I found one grave dating from 1901 where a lad who was only six years of age had been laid to rest. There must have been thirty or forty lads buried in the graves there.

It is hard to believe now but I was sent to Letterfrack because I stole a few toys and a few buns from a shop in Limerick city. Imagine that for a punishment! Nowadays you see drug dealers and murderers going into prison and they are released after a couple of years. Back then people who were only children were locked up and sometimes they had only stolen things in the first place because they were *corribed* with the *crolus* (killed with hunger).

We worked really hard in that reform school making things for the local community. We did tailoring, blacksmithing and all sorts of agricultural work. We even wired mattresses. I remember one job we had to do that was really tough. There was this huge circular pit that you had to climb into. You climbed up through this little window and then you were lowered into the pit. There might be fourteen or fifteen lads lowered into the pit and we had to fan out in a circle. Our job was to stamp on the pile of silage that was in the pit so that the silage would be pressed down as compactly as possible. A farmer would be there organising it and you would have to keep moving and stamping. It was agony because your leg muscles would be aching and ready to collapse, the sweat dripping off you so that the salt was getting into your eyes.

And inside in the school itself punishment was handed out like nobody's business. They beat us with leather straps, really hammered us. Some of the people there were very cruel, unnaturally cruel. That said, not all of them were like that. There were a few who were kind and didn't agree with the corporal punishment. The lads who came from the Travelling community got a real going over sometimes because we were a bit behind in our education compared to the other fellas. They were asking us our sums. 'What's nine nines? What's nine times ten?' and all the rest of it. And we hadn't got a clue what they were talking about. Here we were, Travelling children in off the road and just put into this place without mercy and without an ounce of education. They would ask me 'nine-nines'. I would tell them I didn't know. Then I would be sent to the corner to put out my hands. Then the slaps with the strap on each of my hands. It was sometimes worse again for Traveller children because we had to cope with the jeers of the settled lads. Sometimes you could be called a tinker or a gypsy or a tramp because the other lads knew that we were different and that we hadn't always had the same education that they had. And that was very hurtful too.

The school authorities were trying to force education into us in a hurry. Trying to educate us overnight. And it was the same with the Catechism. Trying to force it into us way too fast. It wasn't right because there was no way that we could take it all in that quickly. It turned a good few of the lads off religion for life. There was no joy in the religion that we were told about in that place.

When I think of those graves in the lonely countryside that is Letterfrack I get very sad. All those poor misfortunates who were buried there and who knew nothing only a life of misery. Many of the same lads' parents were probably dead and they were put into some sort of a home, and maybe they were run out of this home then so that they ended up in an industrial school like Letterfrack. I think Ireland was all crazed up as a country at that time. I don't think the government of the time even knew what it was doing. Everything was confused and mixed up. The country was poor and the government had no money and so they just abandoned all the work of looking after people to the clergy. And what was crazier still was the fact that you could be sent there for the smallest of crimes — stealing food or something. The punishment didn't fit the crime which was a pure sign that those times were a time of confusion for Ireland as a country.

And a good few fellas never recovered properly after their time in there. Surely, their time in there must have affected their minds in some way? Don't ask me how I recovered after my few years in there. Deep down I must be as tough as nails really. Because the truth is that I am after going through the mill. I am after going through the hard mill and I'm only half-way there yet! You could say that I have been going through the mill since the day I was born. I must have about three hundred lines on my face from all of life's worries!

Getting corribed in the Ríspún (Getting beaten in Borstal)

I never saw my parents during the whole of the four years that I spent in Letterfrack although I did get a letter from them every now and then. They were free travelling around Limerick and the southern counties while I was a prisoner inside the walls of the reform school! Like quite a few other lads who were in the reform school I tried to run away. It wasn't such a good idea though because I got one hell of a going-over when I was caught. I ran over twenty-five miles across the mountains in my pyjamas, that is how keen I was to get away from there. I had nothing to eat during my marathon journey and I just drank the water that was in the mountain streams to keep me going. I was really fit back then from playing football in the streets of Limerick and so I made it as far as Westport, in County Mayo, where I was eventually caught. I suppose I was lucky that I didn't disappear in a boghole somewhere, never to be found. The fact that I was used to country living from my family's travelling days was probably what saved me so that I didn't go down a boghole!

I often remember getting some heads of cabbage from the garden and smuggling them into the dormitory to eat. That was how hungry we were, we were happy to chew on the raw cabbage. One night there was another lad there who had smuggled some cabbage in and when the lights went out he put his blanket over his head and started chewing. I was envious at that moment and I was thinking to myself 'I wonder would he ever throw a leaf of cabbage over in my direction!' Within a minute I was glad that he hadn't because the one problem about eating a head of cabbage is that it is a very noisy business. Wasn't your man spotted by one of the Brothers who was wearing a pair of runners. I first heard the tiny squeak coming from his runners as I was sleeping near the door where the Brother had come in. And I said to myself then, 'Your man is dead.' The lad was in a bed not far away from me but there was no way for me to warn him without being seen. The Brother sneaked up on him and started whacking him with the strap and the next thing the poor misfortunate was roaring with pain and fright, the cabbage flying here, there and everywhere.

We were very hungry in that school. But as far as the outside world was concerned we were getting the best of grub! Sometimes a Visiting Committee would come to examine the condition of the school and see that we were well looked after. And lo and behold! What did we get on the day of their visit but the finest of grub. We would receive special meals and we would be kings for a day! We would even get ice cream on that day, something which was a treat then even for children who weren't in an industrial school. When their visit was over however it was back to square one. The leather straps and the cruelty.

There were some punishments that didn't involve physical cruelty. One was when they used to show a picture in the hall of the college that was used as a cinema every month or so. If you were being punished for something your back would be turned to the screen so that you were left only with a good view of the projector! And if you were the punished one you would be sitting there saying 'What's going on now? Did anything happen? Who got shot?' And the other lads would be slagging you because you couldn't see the screen. When I think back on it now I think that it was just very sad that that sort of thing went on. It goes through your heart when you think about it.

There were some of the school authorities who were nice though and don't let anyone tell you any different. I remember one Brother who was very nice and friendly and like me he was mad about sport. I won the cross-country competition there one year—not the day I ran away, mind you! This race had about two hundred lads taking part in it including lads from the local parish of Letterfrack. The competitors were brought up to this mountain called the Diamond and the race was from there back to the industrial school. I remember flying down the hill—because I was as fit as a fiddle then! I can't remember now what the prize was—probably a block of ice cream or something like that! Whatever the prize was, it was definitely worth it at the end of the road anyway.

Leaving Borstal and travelling across the sciuch (water)

After I got out from the Borstal in Letterfrack I headed to England like many of the other former inmates of that industrial school. I needed a change of scene and I needed to try to start afresh in my life. I was only sixteen going on seventeen when I headed over on the boat and up to London. But what did I know about surviving in a huge foreign city like London, having only lived in Limerick, Letterfrack, and the wilds of rural Ireland? I was lost for the first while when I arrived there and like hundreds of other Irish people I spent a time sleeping rough on the streets. I was homeless because I had nowhere to go and because I was so young I didn't know where to start off looking for a job.

I lived for a short while in the Centrepoint Hostel in London and it was while I was there that I made my debut on television! A television company from England came to interview people in the hostel. They interviewed someone from Ireland, England, Scotland and Wales. I was the Irish one and they asked me about what part of Ireland I had come from, what had brought me to London and what life was like for a homeless person in that huge city. I heard later that that folksong with the words 'Let me take you by the hand and lead you through the streets of London . . .' was inspired by that television documentary but I'm not sure whether that is true or not.

The programme brought me some good luck, though, because I managed to get a job and a flat of my own out of it. During my interview I had mentioned that I was good with my hands and a company of wood-joiners named Richardsons contacted the programme and they offered me a job with them. They also provided me with a flat of my own which was a Godsend after so many nights spent freezing out in those cold and dangerous streets under the stars. So I found myself moving from London up to Royston in Barnsley, South Yorkshire where Richardsons had their timber business.

When I was living there the coal pits were operating at full steam. They were using some machines but it was still very dangerous work. It was back-breaking too and the men used to spend long hours down in the darkness and danger of the pits. They were tough people, let me tell you. I have never been in a plane because I don't fancy going high up in the air. In the same way, I didn't feel like getting lost under the ground either and so I decided to give the coalmining a miss and stick to the wood-joining. I was in the construction side of things like so many of the other Irish who emigrated to England at the time and I learnt a lot about timber and the wood-joining business while I was working there.

To have a healthy mind is to have a healthy body; that's what they say. Like any good Limerick man I have always been interested in sport and that was one of the things that I enjoyed the most about living in England. In Ireland you don't see too many Travellers involved in sport on any official level and that is partly because they are discriminated against. Over in Royston, however, it was a different story. The people didn't really mind who you were and I got involved in soccer which I had played as a young fella in the streets of Limerick. I was on the Royston first team and we were top of the league over there. I was as fit as a fiddle.

I stayed in Royston for the best part of a year before upping and coming home to Ireland. I was enjoying the work at Richardsons and they were very good to me but as I explained to them before leaving — I was lonely for home. It was as simple as that. I missed my homeplace and I most of all I missed my family.

Dukkering (Telling fortunes)

I met a few of the Romany Gypsies when I was living over in England. They are lovely people. They have their own language called Romani and their own culture. Some of the women tell fortunes also. The women who tell fortunes are called *durrikers* or *durrigers* in Romany. They have their own style of fortune-telling with the crystal ball and everything. I don't know whether I believe in the fortune-telling myself. I don't know whether it is true or not.

My own mother often told fortunes. She would tell their fortunes to tourists sometimes. On other occasions she might call into a certain house selling some items or *géiging* (begging) and the people of the house might ask her to read their fortune. If you are a Traveller you are an outsider to the settled community and in Ireland the outsider or stranger was always thought to have a special insight that other people don't have.

You would be surprised at how many people believe in fortune-telling today. Sometime a fortune-teller might only be using clever psychology to 'read' someone. The person whose fortune was being told might actually be telling the fortune-teller about themselves unknownst to them and all the fortune-teller would do is repeat that back to them. Then there were other people, other fortune-tellers who might have had a deeper insight—who knows? The fact that I'm a Traveller sometimes means that people ask me to read their fortunes just for the crack. I was asked to read a fellow's palm there in the pub. We were having the crack and this man says to me, 'Willy, will you read my palm? I heard now that you're a *miller* (a great one) for telling the future from someone's palm.' 'Sure I'll have a look for the crack,' I says to him. I looked at his hand. 'Well, I'll tell you something now,' I says, 'you're going to hear good news fairly soon from England.' 'My two daughters are over across,' he says, 'Mary and Rosie. Mary is the eldest.' 'I've never met your daughters, have I?' I says. 'That's right,' says he. I had the conversation going very well now, and I said to this man, 'One of them is going to come back shortly.' 'That's right, Willy,' he says. 'Mary is due back shortly.' What I was trying to do was keep the conversation going with him but at the same time remember what he had said only a few minutes before. Later on in the conversation I mentioned that Mary was the eldest and the man asked me 'How did you know?' Sure, I was after remembering from a while before in our conversation. So the whole thing is a build-up, a sort of a psychology.

Human psychology is a very interesting thing. There are certain unwritten rules there that nearly always come true. I'll give you an example. I asked three people in the bar one day. 'Listen lads, I want each of you to write down a number between one and ten and think of a vegetable at the same time.' All three of them thought of the number seven and of a carrot. Try that out with anyone and you'll find that most people will pick seven, because it's a lucky number. And a carrot is more likely what people think of when they think of a vegetable. They are not going to say 'cabbage' or 'parsnip' or 'onion' for some reason. Seemingly it's the old 'carrot' that always comes out tops. Isn't human nature strange? Strange and wonderful.

The Cant and the Gammon — from the pis (mouths) of the poets

There are many beautiful things about Travellers' culture. One of the most beautiful is our language. Some Travellers call it Cant. Others call it Gammon. It depends on what family you are born into whether you call it Cant or Gammon. Many Traveller families who come from the West of Ireland call the language Cant. Those families who are from the eastern part of Ireland tend to call it Gammon. It is a part of our culture that most Irish people don't know much about. The word Cant comes from the Irish word *caint* which means 'talk' or 'speech'. The word Gammon is also from Irish. It means 'twisted' or 'disguised'. That is because many of the first Travellers were poets who were highly-educated scholars. They were skilled with words and one of their pastimes was to disguise words and twist them around. Sometimes they did this for fun. Other times they did this so that they could speak to each other privately in their own language. This was at the time when Cromwell was massacring Irish people. People forget that Cromwell slaughtered thousands of people including a lot of Travellers. The English hated anyone who travelled for a living whether they were poets, musicians, tinkers or herbalists. They were afraid that Travellers, especially travelling poets, would encourage the people to rise up and rebel against them and so they killed them in their hundreds.

When the Gaelic culture was strong in Ireland the poets were one of the most widely-respected groups in Irish society. They used to travel the country playing music and performing poetry and it was unlucky for anyone to refuse them lodgings. After the Battle of Kinsale in 1601 everything changed for them. The Gaelic princes were gone and the poets could only beg from place to place. A lot of the poets mixed in with all the other different Travellers on the road. There were so many Travellers on the roads at that time, it is hard to know where to start. There were travelling tinsmiths, travelling shoemakers, travelling carpenters, travelling monks, travelling stonemasons, travelling weavers, travelling nailers, travelling musicians and travelling healers. You could go on forever! All of these people were the ancestors of today's Travelling people if you go back far enough.

A different way of tariing (speaking):

The different Travelling families in Ireland all have their own ways of speaking in Cant or Gammon. Different families would have different words for different things. At one time we Travellers had a word for everything in our language but the language isn't as widely known now as it once was.

Some examples of words in Gammon would be:

comra – dog

feen – man

sublia - boy

rabhta – milk

aelum – butter

cullions – potatoes

géger – beggar

durra – bread

Some words that we have were disguised by the Travelling poets in times gone by. The word *laicín* meaning 'girl' is the Irish word *cailín* twisted around. A light is a *glimmer* or a *lodus*, and *lodus* is from the Irish word *solas*. Even the word that describes myself *noiceall-feen* (candle-man) is a word that was disguised by the poets, because it comes from the Irish words *coinneall* and *fian*. Did you ever hear of Fionn and the Fianna? When people look down at Travellers or treat them badly, how many of them realise that they are putting down the culture of the old poets of Ireland?

Travellers would use Gammon for different reasons. Our main language would be English but we would use Cant or Gammon some-times also. Mostly we just use it amongst ourselves because it is our own language and it is a part of us. Some of the scholars say it was a secret language. They are right that Travellers sometimes used the language if they wanted to say something private to other Travellers when settled people were there, but that was not the main reason for using Gammon. Travellers might use the Gammon when they were trading or bargaining with settled people like at the fairs. If they were buying and selling horses from the farmers it was useful to be able to discuss things like the price of a horse privately even while you were in earshot of the farmer. You knew that he probably would not under-stand. Sometimes women would use Gammon amongst themselves when they were calling to the houses to sell items or to *géig* (beg). Sometimes the language was used for privacy.

But one of the main reason Travellers used Gammon was because it was their own language that they had learnt from childhood.

The Gammon táspen? (The Cant dying?)

It is only the old Travellers now who have a good knowledge of our language. As with the Irish language, people neglected the Gammon and a lot of it has been forgotten. I would say there is a big danger nowadays for the Gammon because many Travellers don't use the language anymore. The language is getting less and less in every generation. The Gammon has words in it from Irish, English, French and Latin. As a Travelling people we travelled more widely than the settled community and so our language was influenced by other countries and other Travellers. It is not widely known in Ireland but Irish Travellers have been travelling abroad for hundreds of years.

Some Travellers left Ireland around the time of the Famine and the descendants of these people live in the southern states in America, in places like Georgia and Carolina. Some people like to say that all the Travellers in Ireland are descendants of people who lost their land during the Famine but there is the proof that we are a people with a longer history than that. The Americans have the records to prove that these Travellers came over at the time of the Famine, so us Travellers must have been around well before that time. Many Irish Travellers live and work in other European countries like France, Germany, Sweden, Luxembourg and of course England. Wherever the work is, we will go.

There are some words in our language that come from the Romany language also. The Romany Gypsies have been travelling Europe for centuries and the Irish Travellers would have a lot of contact with the Gypsies in England especially. Some Irish Travellers are married into the Romany Gypsies going back through the generations and so their language has influenced ours and vice versa. Words like *muscer* (garda), *mush* (man) are Romany words that some Irish Travellers would know and use in their own language from time to time. So too are *dukkering* (fortune-telling) or *vardi* (wagon). Some Romany Gypsy families came over to Ireland from Britain during the Second World War and married into the Travelling people here. After that war, many Irish Travellers went to England along with many settled Irish people to help build up those cities that had been destroyed by bombing during the war, cities like Birmingham and Liverpool. Some of these Travellers then stayed in England and married into Gypsy families over there. People who have education talk about how great they are because they can speak a couple of languages like English and Spanish or French and German. The same people don't realise that many of the Travellers who spent only a short while at school can speak a couple of languages whether they be Gammon, Romany, English or German.

The cris nuides (The old people)

There is a lot of talk today about young people being out of control. Some drink too much and take drugs and then they get violent. When I was growing up things were different in both the Travelling and settled communities. Your parents and grandparents were very strict with you as a child and you learnt to respect them. To disrespect an older person was taken as a very serious thing. Take my father now as an example. He was a very strict man, may he rest in peace. You would do what he said and that was the end of it. There was no such thing as using bad language either. The four-letter word didn't exist. You couldn't say it and that was a fact. The parents would threaten that they would drag you before a priest if you said one foul word. 'We'll bring you to a priest now,' they'd say. 'And he'll put you in a barrel and you won't be able to come out of it!'

They had the life frightened out of you but it worked! There was no vulgarity like there is today. Today the vulgar words are very common — even on the television! They are even inventing new four-letter words that we have never heard before! There must have been different ways of getting angry in the old days but I don't remember all this cursing, that's for sure. Now you turn on the radio, the television and all you hear is this cursing. I call the television the divil's box because half of it is unnatural. I only watch television the odd time. I like the Irish-language station the best because it has a lot of documentaries about Irish culture and rural life. I can't understand much of the Irish but I like the sight of all those country scenes. I like the Irishness of that station and all the old scenes including the thatched houses and the currachs.

No Mincéir anásha (No Travellers here)

We respected our parents but everyone else didn't unfortunately. Sometimes they would bang the *rodas* (door) in your face. I would see that very sad look come over my mother's face. She would be hurt, really hurt to the core and it is impossible to explain that feeling to someone who has never experienced it. Even when I was with her at the *jiggers* (doors) of the *céns* and I only three or four years of age, it didn't stop some people from being hurtful. I remember people telling me to 'feck off' or 'we don't want any Travellers here', and all the rest of it. It would make my mother very upset and sometimes she would get very cross. When she got cross then she would take it out on me! But she would

never have cursed anyone back. She would never believe in stooping
to the same level as the person who had been rude to her.

Getting lerky (angry)

Sometimes I feel very bitter about the way Travellers were treated in
Ireland. When I was younger I sometimes hoped that I could just
disappear out of this country. In my mind I used to wish that someone
would kidnap me so that I could escape from some of this hardship!
And it nearly happened too! There was an American couple down
around the Carlton Cinema here in Limerick one evening when I was
only five or six years of age and playing the mouth organ. And they
wanted to take me away. It was touch and go for a few minutes I can tell
you! I was thinking to myself 'Will I go or not?! I could be a rich man in
the future. I could be living in Honolulu, or somewhere!' And this elderly
couple were there and they trying to persuade me to come away to
America with them. They were asking me about myself and there was a
big pile of newspapers and an old box beside me and I said to them —
'That is where I sleep!' And I played an old tune for them on the mouth
organ! They were mad to take me away as they had no children
themselves. I couldn't go with them in the end though because I got
that lonesome feeling. And before they finished talking to me they gave
me twenty-five or thirty dollars which was a lot of money back then!
And they brought me some sweets or some candy as they called it! I
didn't know what candy was when they first asked me would I like
some — to me sweets were sweets.

I had a habit for going to the pictures, an addiction you could say. I
was always heading to the pictures. Any money I had made during the
day singing and playing music would get spent on filling my small belly

in front of the silver screen. I would go away and buy two boiled crubeens (pig's toes). You could buy them in the shops at that time whereas nowadays they are very scarce. I used to get two crubeens, two bags of chips and four bars of chocolate. And I'd have the whole lot hidden under my jumper! And I'd go into the pictures (cinema) because I was mad for pictures. The only problem was that when I ate all of that food I would fall asleep inside in the cinema! And I wouldn't see the picture at all!

One night I went into the pictures and I fell asleep. When I woke up the whole picture-house was cleared and I was on my own in the dark. Now I have slept in some queer places in my time. I have even slept in a few graveyards. But this place was the most frightening place I have ever been! At least in a graveyard you can see the sky or the moon. In the picture-house once the lights are off you are in absolute darkness. Darkness so pitch-black that you can't even see your hand in front of your face! Well, I got a serious panic attack I can tell you. I jumped over chairs, left, right and centre, fell over chairs and down steps, I nearly broke my leg! Eventually I managed to find my way out. It was a while before I ate that much grub again on my way to the picture-house, I can tell you!

The grís (inspiration) for painting

The joy of it is what inspires me to paint. The joy of creating a new landscape. The chance to create beauty. God gave you and me this beauty and yet man seems intent on destroying it. Eventually it will all be gone. Eventually. In years to come there will be paintings here and there of the bullfinch, the linnet, and a range of other little birds. And the children not yet born will see these paintings and they will say 'What's that bird there?' because the chances are they will never have seen one of them. Birds the like of that may have disappeared from the earth by then. Because man is destroying the earth, whatever pollution we are pumping up there into the sky. It's like the cuckoo. You can hardly hear ever the cuckoo these days at all. You can never hear the corncrake. He's gone. Eventually all the little birds—I paint them because I love them and I love painting nature—eventually they will be gone and it will be man who will have destroyed it. And all you will have left is a painting or a photograph of these creatures.

I find great joy in them. You can get the details of each bird into your paintings, the colours. Even painting the land that made us—all that nature while it is still there. Ireland is only a small little nation. You can imagine this land in about two hundred years' time. It will be full. You might get an odd park in the city here and there if you are lucky. But the old landscape is gone. You might see a mountain alright but there will be houses going up towards that mountain! You might see the very top of it! But on the valleys it will be all gone. Strange isn't it. Right down to the edge of the sea! They are even getting greedy now—because they want the beauty—they want to live right beside the sea. They want a new house beside the sea, they want another house above in Dublin, they want another house over where their office is. Man, will you stop! It's all greed. Land-greed. All I want is a house outside the city for my kids where I could live in peace and quiet. I don't want two houses or three houses. One will do. With plenty of rooms of course–for my grandchildren! I want a combined hospital—the Cauley hospital!

My gálias (children) and Limerick city

A NEWBORN CHILD

Blinking stars shine high above
The moon beams through breaking clouds
A newborn child gives out its first cry
For the Lord has given
This child a life
Its parents glow with such delight
And grandparents look to the very sky
To give praise, to the Man on High.

I have seven children, thank God. One of my children has already passed on, God be good to her. We lost our eldest child Julie-Anne who died of pneumonia a few years ago. We had a caravan up on the canal bank, right on the edge of the Shannon in the heart of the city here. We lived there for fourteen years and she died of pneumonia while we were there. After she died we were given a house but unfortunately it came too late for her. And to tell you the truth, life in the caravan was probably healthier even though it was dangerous for the children to be so close to the river. The house in which we live since is falling down.

A housing committee has visited us and taken photographs of the house, photos of the dampness and the cracks in the walls. You can't do anything with the house. You can't put wallpaper up because it's going to fall down. Even the lino there has dampness coming up through it. The whole house is just complete damp-rot. I have to cover my walls with my paintings. Half the cracks are hidden by my paintings!

My daughter died when she was only seventeen, the poor little girl. May the Lord have mercy on her. She used to go to Lisnagry, a special place for children who are disabled. She was in a wheelchair for many years. They brought her back when she was dying and we put her into the caravan. Fourteen years on the edge of the canal and only after she had died did we finally move into a house. My wife, like myself, was devastated when our daughter died. Life is tough, that's for sure.

My children are named Rosemary, Lily, Noreen, William, Thomas, Winnie and Mags. The two last little girls are twins. There's just one of my daughters married so far. Her name is Lily and she lives in London where she is married to a foreign man. She is very happy with him and I am also a grandfather so I couldn't be happier. I hope that someday Lily and her husband will come back to live in Ireland. I don't know whether she likes the life in England but I suppose in a way she has no choice but to live there. There's no place available back here. And her husband feels settled over there for the time being although he told me he wouldn't mind coming to live in Ireland. He's a very decent fella and he phones up every now and then and asks me to come over. But I don't like going on planes so I tell him I'll stay put until they visit next. 'I'm here to stay now,' I tell him. And I wouldn't like travelling over there anyway, not at this stage of my life. I'm here to stay now, this is my nation. This is my land.

Leaving the helm (city)

I would prefer to get my children out of the city of Limerick. They don't really like the city at all. I'm just waiting and hoping for the best, hoping that I get a house out the country. I'd like to go around Newport or somewhere like that. I still love Limerick but it's not the same city that it was when I was young. I am sorry to say that but I suppose many people in other Irish cities could say the same thing if they were honest about it. There is too much violence in our cities, especially at night. People have too much to drink and they get all tanked up and ready to fight whoever they meet. I'm always afraid for my children if they are ever out late at night.

And the worst of it is that deep down in the centre of my heart I still love Limerick as much as any man who was born and bred in this city. When I was young and we were on the move, my favourite sight was to see the lights of the city as we came back in over the Shannon in our horse-drawn caravan. I have very fond memories of coming over the bridge and back into the city at Christmas-time after a spell out the country. I knew that the excitement and bustle of Christmas was about to begin and that I could make a right few shillings playing the different carols and ballads on my mouth organ. It is true to say that deep down everyone loves their hometown. There is an urge there in every man and woman to return to their hometown no matter how long they have been away. At the end the memories that shaped them belong to that hometown and so they can never really be separated from it.

> Crystal waters I do hear
> Flowing around your Abbey shores
> And down by John's Castle
> Where there was many a battle
> In gone-by days, gone-by days.
> When I was a boy
> With my hobnail boots
> I'd run up the alleyways
> And across to John's Square
> With the bells ringing out.

For this is New Year's Day
In Limerick so dear and dear
Where all are joyful,
And children at play,
And old folks having a cheer,
So merry, so merry and fair
Is Limerick on this joyful day.
Will they remember me,
My Limerick folk
As I walk along with an easy stride
With a painting hanging from my side
And I whistling a merry tune
In this dear city of mine?

Frog–collecting — a lesser-known Traveller trade!

Travellers have always been able to turn their hands to anything. If you go back through the history books you'll find mentions of us working at hundreds of different trades You name it, we could turn our hands to it whether it was peddling, fortune-telling, metalworking, selling feathers, fruit harvesting, fixing china, selling horsehair or poitín-making. Here is another trade now to add to that list — frog-collecting!

I was a frog-collector when I was a young lad and we were living in the Newport area of County Tipperary. I used to collect a bag of frogs and I'd bring them to McCormacks' bar in Newport and there was a woman there who would give me a half-a-crown for each bag of frogs that I collected. She had timber barrels down in the cellar of the pub and she would put all the frogs into the barrels and as soon as the barrels were full she would seal them up and send them off to France. She was making a fortune from it I believe. Frogs' legs are a delicacy in

France and people pay top dollar for that meal in places like Paris. So I had a great old business going at one stage, wandering the fields and bogs, grabbing the frogs and popping them into bags. Hop-a-long Willy, I should have been known as! And when I had my pence gathered together it was off to the pictures for me to see the latest western or whatever happened to be showing. All those frogs collected and sent across the water so that I could go and see John Wayne on the big screen!

Window-cleaning

I worked as a window-cleaner in Limerick for a while. The Saint Vincent de Paul came down and they asked myself and my two brothers whether we were interested in going window-cleaning. What happened was they gave us a trial from the Labour Exchange. But there was some kind of a mix-up and our dole was cut off and we ended up having to pack in the window-cleaning. They were supposed to arrange it so that we could keep a percentage from the window-cleaning and claim some dole for the days we weren't working but the whole thing never really got organised. We never succeeded in that business venture, although we were really hoping that we would. We were hoping that we would someday have our own van, with *Cauley and Co., Window-cleaners,* on the side of it. It's about thirty years ago now this—well before I started painting. If I only knew then, what I know now! I could have been painting landscapes and making some few quid, some few bob.

Catching the iascáns (Catching fish)

I don't travel much today. We just go off for holidays — to Ballybunion, Kilkee, Lahinch, Spanish Point. It is not the same as the roving life in times gone by. We go off for a drive in the van. You're still not free though. It's not like the old days. It's a routine. Go out there and come back here. I brought my young lads out camping a few times and we camped by the lakes. We did some fishing. I taught them how to do the night-lining that my father had taught me.

It's the same thing as eel-poking. You get a small bit of a stick that's about a foot in length. And you have your line about an inch or two from the top of the stick. You slit your line down through the stick and attach your worm and your hook. Then you go under a bridge where the water is and poke the top of your stick into the water. Hold your fishing line — the bit of gut — in your left hand and poke the stick in through the slits of the bridge and the eel will grab it. Then you let go of your stick and put out your line and you have your eel. The river eels are the best because they are the cleanest. We would boil them first and then eat them. They say that the eel is the cleanest fish in the sea or the river because he doesn't eat any rubbish. And the funny thing is — they say that the trout is the dirtiest!

Fishing at night-time can be fun too. You can have a nightline with a bait and hook. On the river you look and check where the heavy flow moves into a calm patch of water and where that flow comes out again. That is where you should locate your stick. Stick it right down in that gap between the quick and the slow water. You should put a small bit of a weight on the stick and keep it as close as possible to the bank, well-stuck into the ground. The trout comes along the bank looking for his dinner. He slides along at the edge of the water scouting out for worms or bugs and he gets tempted by your bait.

Sure, I was the only man that fished from his window in Annacotty — from a caravan! We had a caravan under Annacotty bridge at one time. The same area has become all built up since, but we had the side of our caravan facing the river. And I would have my window open during the day. Early in the morning I would wade across through the water and put down my line right under the archway of the bridge. That's the spot where the fish and the eels come in to rest. And I would have one weight there at the end, about two foot down under the water. And I would leave it there and walk back across the water and bring my line in through the window. And then I would watch *Bosco* on television while fishing from the window. On the commercial breaks I would bring the eels in and throw them in the pan! Just like that. Not a bother! We would be watching *Bosco* on a black and white television, off a battery. I would have a mug of tea in my hand. And when I saw the movement on the line I would pull in as fast as I could. You would have to do it with speed, otherwise the line would get tangled. And my wife would chop up the fish and throw them in the pan for our supper! Then we'd all go back to watching *Bosco* again. The life of Reilly!

Snaring the sceiv (fish)

You can catch, eels, trout, fluke — all sorts of different fish using a nightline. You never know what you're going to find on the end of the line when you haul it in. There's a technique in it. There is also a technique whereby you can actually snare a fish using copper wire, believe it or not! It is done in much the same way as you would snare a rabbit. Snaring a rabbit is cruel but when I was young the hungry times meant that you had no choice sometimes. A rabbit in the pot was survival.

Snaring a trout or a salmon is done with copper wire, something that the tinsmith might have handy. There is a special way of shaping the copper snare. You would go and stand right next to a falls, right next to the noise of the crashing water. My habit was to put three snares, three circles with baits very close to one another. All of the snares would be attached to a very strong stick in beside a low bank if at all possible.

And you would have to try and nab the fish when the flow at the falls wasn't at its strongest, where the falls come down off one bank before its journey onto the next. If you are lucky the snare will grip the fish when he makes his way over the first bank. With this type of fishing you would need a good heavy rock leaning on the top of your stick at the riverbank. When a salmon or a trout is jumping they are all muscle and if your stick isn't secure they won't be trapped.

If they get into the snare however you can normally start licking your chops and looking forward to your dinner. The snare is designed in such a way that the more the fish struggles, the tighter the grip of the snare.

Pictures in my liart (mind)

I have loved singing and music from the moment that I was born. I may have even loved it before I was born as they say now that the unborn baby can hear and respond to music when they are in the womb! My mother was always singing so I probably popped out into the world with a rake of tunes learnt off and ready to go! I like the old-style tenors, the likes of Josef Locke and John McCormack. I also like traditional music, music by groups like Ryan's Fancy. They are a Tipperary group who emigrated to Canada and are still very big over there. I like The Barleycorn and The Drifters too. There is a tune by The Furey Brothers who were also Travelling people that's lovely too. It's called *The Lonesome Boatman.* I often whistled that tune for friends in pubs. It's a unique tune, a haunting sound and it inspires me in my painting. The way the tune comes bending in on you, the whistles, like a landscape coming into view — it has an atmosphere all of its own. It puts pictures in my mind because it reminds me of a caravan down on marsh land somewhere. That's the image that comes to my mind. Or else a lonely quay somewhere with a few empty boats tied up near the rocks.

I have always loved films and like many Travellers I've always been fond of westerns. Some of the westerns are the best films that were ever made. The kids love them too because of the horses and all the action. There was a kind of a romantic film made a few years ago about the Travelling life called *Into the West* which was a good film. I love detective stories too and the way that they sift through all the clues to sort the mystery out. Sometimes when I'm half-dreaming to myself I imagine that I'm a private detective myself! I was passing one of my neighbours' houses one day and I was talking to myself after watching some detective film or other, the way you do when you think no-one is listening to you.

I was pretending to myself that I was a private detective — that I was Columbo and all the rest of it. And I was saying, 'Will you answer the question, Ma'am?' which was one of the lines from the programme. 'Are you sure you were there, Ma'am?' I was saying to myself in a New York accent. And my neighbour heard me as I passed their gate and she said to me—'Are you alright there?' So I had to cover up for myself. 'Oh, yeah,' says I. 'I was just thinking to myself there for a moment!' The embarrassment of it. Ohhhh! There's nothing worse than getting caught when you're half-dreaming to yourself. Isn't it true?

THE MEMORY TREE

When a tree grows old
It falls and dies
Through years it stood
With branches of many
Leaves of beautiful green
And in autumn of brown and gold.
Through summers gone by
We sat beneath the old oak tree
Pastime stories were told
To rest for a while
Beneath the tree
And the meadows in full bloom.
Many's a picnic we had then
On those long summer days
With all our blessed friends
The young ran wild and wild
Around that tree
A tree of memories
But now it is gone
That old oak tree
And many, many
A friend, so true.

The Candlelight Painter—how my dhíls got that minic (How I got that name)

I think it was Maureen Sparling, the poet, who originally called me 'the candlelight painter'. When the kids were asleep I would paint away by candlelight, and that was the way that the name started building up. Eventually the whole city started calling me 'the candlelight painter'. The newspapers—the *Limerick Post* and the *Limerick Leader*—started calling me that. At the moment now, I am the Limerick painter. A fellow came down to me one day and he had a Christmas box for me. And I thought it was something good. 'Twas only a box of candles! And he said to me, 'You won't stop painting now, boy.'

I used to pull out two candles every night and light them. I even went on fire one night. My hair. I was leaning over the candle a bit much, and I was a small bit drunk to be honest with you, and the next thing my hair went off on fire. And my wife was saying me, 'You're on fire, you're on fire!' And I was saying 'Where? Where?' 'The top of your head, you fool!' She was lying on the bed in the caravan and she saw me going up in flames! I had to keep a wet towel on top of my head for the best part of a week. Lying flat on the bed with a wet towel on my head!

Bringing Ireland and my ríb (hair) with them

I met an Irish couple one night and they asked me to paint a picture for them before the morning because they were heading back to the USA the next day. They were sad about leaving Ireland again and they wanted to bring an image of the 'old country' with them. So I told them I would and welcome. The only problem was that I discovered that I had no canvas left. So when I got home I got out a white shirt that I had. I cut it up and I stretched it over a board and managed to make a small canvas out of that. Well, I started working feverishly because I wanted to make sure I had the painting completed by morning. I'd had a few drinks for inspiration and as I was leaning over the canvas my hair went up in flames (again!) I lost a valuable piece of property in the process! It was a case of a wet towel and a week hiding inside the house again. I was probably lucky it wasn't worse!

Unfortunately, I was in such pain that I didn't get to complete that painting and that couple had to go back to the States without it. I sent them a message early the next morning apologising to them and explaining the situation. I'm sure that they forgave me. Over the years a few of my paintings have gone across the water, but to tell the truth I would have preferred if they had stayed in Ireland. Each man's work should stay in their own country if at all possible. That's my opinion anyway.

THE CANDLELIGHT PAINTER

The candles a'flickering
Throughout the night
My paint brush a'swaying
From left to right
My painting in colour
Is coming to life
Though weary and tired
I must proceed
To finish this painting
Before this very night
My inspiration is strong

And my mind a'willing
Nothing must go wrong
Excitement beholds me
This creation of life
And to me it seems
A pleasant sight
With colours ablaze
From the flickering light
But now I must rest
A painter am I
I've done my very best.

ANOTHER LIFE?

With outstretched hands
You received me, my Lord
From this lonely life of mine
With your teardrop upon my cheek
Your heart pounding with mine
And you, with your bleeding wounds
Had saved your pain for me
With opened Heaven gates
You let me enter
For your kingdom is sweet and free
And you are the one
The only one
That stopped to save me
A lonely and sad sinner like me.

I was often asked if I was born again what would I like to be. Well, the first thing that comes to my mind is a swan. Yes, I know it's a strange thing to say but I have my own reasons for that answer. When you look at how peaceful a creature the swan is it seems to have no worries, it comes and goes as it pleases. And most of all it has rights. No one tells it to move on, no one tries to control it. So there you have it, my friend. Peace and freedom. That's all that I wish for in life. I came into this life peaceful and I intend to go peacefully. Just leaving my name behind me because no matter how tough your life is you always turn to God in the last minutes. It is said you must be like a child to enter the Kingdom of God.

I wonder are there any halting sites for the Travellers up in Heaven because if there are they must be a sight better than the ones here on earth. The ones down here are like Long Kesh. And the walls keep getting higher and higher. Out of sight, out of mind. Every country has different peoples with different cultures. Who is to say that one people or one culture is better than the other? Who is to say that one people are more perfect than another? Are we not equal in the eyes of God? We are all just here on this earth for a very short while and isn't it better to leave this life with a clean soul, leaving your love behind to all mankind, the whole human race, your brothers and sisters.

Stéis (The end)

Four *scéalta*

A Frightful Experience

A long time ago, away back in Connemara in the far, far West of Ireland there was an old man with his donkey, his cart and tent. Old Christy Donovan was one of those rare tinker lads. Most of his life he had been a loner and mostly camped on lonesome roads. Old Christy was never a man for company. He would sit beside his campfire till all hours of the morning, singing and humming away to himself. His little dog would listen away. He looked over at the little dog called Tiny.

'You and me, Tiny,' he said, 'will die at the side of the road and no-one will even know that we lived on this earth at all. Do ye know something, Tiny? You just lay there on the ashes and you say nothing. It's a pity dogs don't talk,' he muttered.

Tiny just kept staring at his old master wondering if he was losing his mind. Now and again a rat would appear from the ditch and Tiny would rush to catch him. 'Go and get him, Tiny!' Old Christy would shout. 'Get him for Dadda, old stock, for I won't sleep a wink tonight if that rat is on the loose.'

And so the night became morning. Old Christy slept outside his tent that night. Finally he opened his eyes to a cold and frosty morning.

'Are you alive, Tiny?' he asked as he poked his dog. 'It's time to tackle up and move on. There's too many rats around here,' he muttered. 'Come on, move our bones.'

And so they moved on, wandering down the narrow lane, Tiny walking beside his master's feet. Old Christy would wipe his hard, old face. 'I would love a sup of tea, Tiny.'

The sweat poured down from beneath his old cap. 'There's no good in smoking this old pipe, Tiny, I have no tobacco.' From time to time, Old Christy would pick up old autumn leaves. He would crunch them up and stuff them into his pipe and when he took that first puff from his pipe, you could hear him coughing across the valley. 'Ye should see me lungs, Tiny,' he would say. 'They are as black as the ace of spades.'

Once more they arrived at a new camping ground. Old Christy untackled his donkey and put up his tent. He lit up the fire and finally put his old gallon of water on it. He had got three eggs from the last house he begged at. And he put them into the gallon of water. When the eggs were done he gave one to Tiny. 'If I had another spoon, I would give it to you, Tiny,' he joked. 'Anyway, aren't you lucky I peeled off the shell for you.'

The night arrived. The moon was full with dark skies covering its places. Old Christy was weary and tired and so he entered his tent and lay there upon the straw. But it was not for long as he felt something move up the leg of his pants. 'My Jasus!' he screamed. 'What's that?' He put down his hand to grip it. Sure enough it was a rat. Christy was screaming around the road and at the same time gripping the rat inside the leg of his pants. 'You cowardly dog, Tiny,' he shouted. 'Did you take a sleeping pill or something?' All around the camp fire he hopped wondering how to get the rat out of his pants. 'Oh, mother, please help!' he shouted. 'Tiny,' he roared, 'you were supposed to protect me. It must be the egg I gave you. That's the last egg you'll get off me, Tiny.'

Christy knew that if he took away his hand from the rat he would climb further up the leg of his pants. So there was only one thing to do. Unbuckling his belt he pulled down his pants taking his left leg out. He held on to the rat in the other and slowly took his pants off.

All around the road he beat his pants off the road. 'Come out ye devil,' he shivered and screamed. He knew he could not throw his pants into the fire for it was the only one he had. Tiny, the dog just lay there with one ear up and the other down. But shortly later, the rat made a dash out of his pants. Old Christy was so delighted. 'Do ye see, you, Tiny?' He pointed. 'I'm going to swap you if it's the last thing I do. The next village I come to, I'm going to get rid of ye and I hope they don't give ye an egg like I did, ye cowardly dog ye! What are ye, Tiny? You're a cowardly dog!'

Mistaken Identity

There were two farmers one time. Neither of them could get on together. They even cheated on one another. When Simpson knew that O'Hare was asleep, he would go across the fields to take some bales of hay from O'Hare's barn and O'Hare's dog would not bark for he knew Simpson quite well. And this was going on for years. Each of them would do something wrong to the other from time to time. For instance, O'Hare knew what time that Simpson would go to Mass on a Sunday. For Old Simpson had to pass O'Hare's house to get to church. And each Sunday, he would listen from inside the hedge and sure enough he would hear the sound of the trap and pony going by. He also knew tht no-one would be at Simpson's house, only the sheep dog and that dog also knew O'Hare.

'Now what could I take here,' he would ask himself. 'Let me think, now,' he would say. Opening the sack he grabbed two ducks and a chicken and shoved them down into the sack and away with him across the fields.

Johnny and Molly came back from Mass that morning and Molly looked around the yard feeling something unusual. 'Johnny,' she said, 'the ducks didn't come out to greet us, don't you think that's unusual? 'Be god an' ye're right, Molly. What in the blazes could have happened to them? Even our best laying hen is gone. O'Hare!' he shouted. 'Steady on now, Johnny,' Molly would say, 'sure it might have been a fox that took them.' 'Oh, no, it's O'Hare alright, he's getting his own back on me.' 'Sure, what are ye saying Sonny? Did ye do something wrong on him?' 'Ah, never mind woman,' he bellowed.

Down at the pub that night there were quite a few there. At each end of the counter were the two lads, O'Hare at one end and Simpson at the other. The rest of the folk knew the story between these two men. They knew for years. And it was only a matter of time before it blew over.

Both of them gave a sneary eye at the other. O'Hare would shout out, 'Someone must have been short of hay this year, God help us.' 'Oh yes, indeed,' Simpson would reply, 'someone must be starving with the hunger,' thinking about his ducks and chicken.

And these comments were going on for most of the night, from hay to ducks, from ducks to hay. Then, suddenly a loud shout came from across the room. It was Fr Kelly. Kelly was a strict priest. He would remind you of a Viking, with the big beard on him and as strong as you could get them. 'I'm sick of people in this parish arguing with one another so I'm going to say this only once: if ye don't make amends now, then ye won't be welcome in my church. You act like a pack of 'ould wolves.'

Well things did quieten down for a while. But of course it was not for long and it all blew up on a fine summer's day. Simpson had gone to the fair one morning. He brought some fowl and vegetables and an old goat to sell or trade. And at the end of the day, things were sold and things were bought. As Simpson was about to leave he spotted this donkey beside the pub and ended up buying him. In the meantime back at O'Hare's farm, O'Hare was around the yard looking for his donkey. 'Now where could he be gone to?' he had asked himself throughout the day. He searched his land all over but no trace of his donkey. And so he came to this crossroads and lo and behold, but who was coming up the road? Yes, I'm afraid it was Simpson with his pony and cart, and his new donkey. O'Hare's eyes burned with rage, his face all red. He tore at Simpson with a mighty temper. 'My donkey!' he roared. 'What are ye doing with my donkey?' 'What are ye talking about man?' Simpson screamed. Well, up and down the road, the two of them tore at each other.

And coming toward them with her hands outstretched was Mrs O'Hare. 'Paddy, Paddy,' she shouted. 'I have found our donkey up in O'Sullivan's farm!' Well, the two boys stood there staring at each other for once in their lives. Did they ever see two donkeys that looked like twins! They both laughed, shook hands and were at peace at last!

The Barn Owl

The house was old and thatched and the cobbled stone passage was winding its way towards it — it was the kind of house where Peter would be welcomed. The rose bushes climbed around the old house; anyone who grows flowers, he thought, must have a generous heart. The upper part of the half-door was open suggesting that this was a welcoming house. 'God bless the house,' Peter shouted out, 'and God save all here.' He often heard his parents speak these blessing words.

An old lady came to the door wearing an old black shawl. 'What do you want?' the old lady asked. 'God bless you, mam, could I be bothering you for a piece of bread and jam, missus?' She looked at him with blinking eyes, but friendly. 'Where in God's name did you come from?' she asked, 'because the lane leading to my house is a fair bit to the main road.' 'Well, missus, I came across the land you see, and it's the shortest way to get to a house.' 'I see,' said the old woman. 'I suppose you're a tinker lad?' 'That be so, mam,' Peter replied. 'My parents are far away.' 'And how far away would that be, lad?' 'A couple of hundred miles or so,' he replied. 'My God, child, what do they think?' 'Oh, they are used to me, Mam.' 'You must be worn out, you poor fella.' 'I'm a bit tired alright, mam.' 'Alright, come you in, sit down yonder and I'll fill you out a bit of dinner.'

Peter was happy to hear this. His belly would be full soon. He was looking at the size of the old pot, and wondering how she was able to lift it from the open fire. It was a peaceful old house. The old woman pointed at the pot. 'Do you see that pot, me lad? Well that pot, my lad, fed twelve of my children. Oh, but that was long ago. Now they are all in America, God bless them. I don't even know how many grandchildren I have, for I seem to have lost count. Anyway you get that dinner inside ye, and I hope you stay the night, for I haven't talked to a human soul in a long time. When you're finished I'll introduce you to an old friend of mine.' 'Is it your husband, Mam?' Peter asked. 'Oh indeed, yes. He passed away ages ago. Oh, you will like my old friend. Wait and you'll see.' Moments later she took Peter by the hand and led him out to the barn. 'Now look up there, lad. Do ye see that large beam up there?' 'Yes indeed, Mam,' said Peter. 'I see an owl up there.' 'Oh, that's no ordinary owl, lad. That owl is my dear sweet husband.' 'But I thought you said he was dead, mam?' 'Oh yes, indeed he is dead lad. It's just that he has come back as an owl. Back to protect me, do you see, lad?' Peter kept staring at the owl. 'Well, missus, if you think that it is he, then let it be so. Whatever makes you happy.' A teardrop fell from her saddened eyes. 'Some day, I too will be an owl and I'll lay perched up on there beside him.' Peter looked at her and said, 'But what about Heaven?' 'My lad,' she spoke, 'This is my Heaven, this is where all my memories are.'

The following morning he woke to find a silent house. There was no trace of the old woman. He began to leave and then turned back to stroll towards the barn. Two owls lay perched on the beam.

The Chimney Sweep

Jimmy the Poker, he was named. The Poker was a chimney sweep by trade, and his father, and his father before him. All sweepers. It was a good trade. Of course, that was if you did it right. And so it was, the Poker was the best at his trade. Every day he would tie his brushes and sticks or rods onto his bike and away he'd go for the whole day. The Poker had a habit of buying two bottles of stout from the local pub, and on his journey he would take a drink from time to time.

He had a shirt on him and, God knows, it must have been on him a lifetime. And you could say the same for all the rest of his clothes. Everything about him was black. The only thing that was clean was his eyes. His eyes were as white as snow. And if he walked towards you in the dark, you would think a pair of eyes were coming at you, eyes without a body, eyes cycling with a bike. I'd say in his days he would have given many a person a fright as he came home in the dark.

Even a rat wouldn't take a bit of him for all they'd taste is soot or ashes. But the Poker wasn't the one to bother about his looks. Once he had a few bob in his pocket, he was a happy man. Many's the pub he entered and cleaned the chimneys for a pint or two. Saving money was not his way. Oh no. Not the Poker. He had often said that if he died and left his money behind him — 'sure the priest would get it or the undertaker and where then would that leave me?' The priest would get a few bottles of wine and the other fella would get drunk for himself or a get a bag of oats for his carriage horse.

They say that if you touch a chimney-sweep on the shoulder that you will have luck for the day. So it happened one day, as the story goes. This bank owner knew of the Poker. The banker saw him coming down the street, swaying this way and that way, drunk of course. But it didn't bother the banker. So he reached out and touched The Poker on the shoulder, hoping he'd have a bit of luck. But The Poker, noticed, as drunk as he was—'God blast you man,' he roared. 'You should have asked my permission to touch me. And for that you didn't—that you may have bad luck for the year.' And so, believe it or not, the following week the banker went bankrupt.

One morning the Poker opened his eyes only to find that he had a splitting headache. 'Oh my God,' he grunted. 'I must get some money somewhere, I must get the price of a cure.' Up and down the village he plodded, grumbling, grunting, swearing, thinking where would he get money. He just had to have a drink. He came to Murphy's Bar. He went in. 'How's it going, Tim?' he said to the barman. 'Well, Poker,' Tim Murphy replied, 'looking at you, I'd say I'm doing fine, thank you.' The Poker leaned over the counter and said, 'Mr Murphy, will you do me one turn please?'

And so he did. Murphy turned around once. 'Do you want me to turn around again?' Murphy said, jokingly. 'Arra, stop the messing Murphy. Give me a drink on the book, that's the good boy.' 'Sorry, no can do,' replied Murphy. 'But for God's sake man, have ye no pity at all, at all?' 'I have only pity for myself, my dear Poker.' Poor old Poker stood there with bloodshot eyes, and he glared at Murphy and said, 'Well, Murphy, I wish you bad luck for the year.'

Now, when Murphy heard this, the sweat poured down his cheeks. Especially when he remembered what he had heard about the banker and the bankruptcy. So Murphy bent down and took up some bottles of stout and said to Poker. 'If I give you these three bottles, will you go and never come into my pub again? And will you break the curse you put upon me?' The Poker looked at him and said, 'Well Murphy, could you possibly make it five bottles and ten cigarettes?'

Murphy stood there shocked. 'Well, Poker,' Murphy said, 'I've seen greed all my life, but you beat the biscuit. You put a curse on me, Poker. Well I'm putting a curse on you. Not only one, but half a dozen of them. That you may never get a drink again. That your bike may get punctured a thousand times a year and that its chain snaps in a hundred places. And finally, that your chimney rods and brushes may never reach the chimney pots.'

Well, Poker looked at him with amusement. 'By God, Murphy,' he said, 'I never knew that you could curse a person. So, I'll tell you what I'll do. Could we both break the curses. And you give me the deal you made the first time.' 'And what's that?' Murphy asked. Poker put up three fingers, saying 'Three bottles of stout, my good man.' Murphy pushed him towards the door and shoved him out, saying 'I wouldn't give you Holy Water to bless yourself, you devil.'